DEMOCRACY AND THE OCCULT

DEMOCRACY AND THE OCCULT

PHILIP J. GENTLESK

Democracy and the Occult
© 2024 by Philip J. Gentlesk

Scriptures marked NIV are taken from the NEW INTERNATIONAL VERSION (NIV): Scripture taken from THE HOLY BIBLE, NEW INTERNATIONAL VERSION ®. Copyright© 1973, 1978, 1984, 2011 by Biblica, Inc.TM. Used by permission of Zondervan

Printed in the United States of America.
ISBN-13: 979-8-9906415-0-1- Paperback
979-8-9906415-1-8- Hardcover
LCCN: xxxx

Royal Crest Publishing
Waxhaw, North Carolina

Royal Crest
PUBLISHING

CONTENTS

CHAPTER ONE

LIFE IN THE DISUNITED STATES

Every day, millions of schoolchildren across the United States start their day by reciting the Pledge of Allegiance.

Their young voices are filled with excitement as they honor the flag of "the United States of America, one nation, under God, indivisible, with liberty and justice for all."

These days, the words about our "indivisible" nation ring hollow.

We live in a country divided.

In fact, I am almost 80 years old, and I have never seen the American people as divided as they are right now. Some say that the United States is more polarized than it has been at any time in its history, with the exception of the Civil War. And I believe they are right.

Tempers seem hotter than ever before. Arguments are louder. Grudges last longer. Feelings are hurt easier.

I recently spoke to a friend who told me that he used to look forward to family get-togethers, but not anymore.

These days, those once-friendly conversations over dinner are turning into shouting matches. Almost always, someone stomps out of the house in anger and goes home early. What were once love feasts have become free-for-alls.

Why? What has happened to cause such animosity between family members and friends? And what can we do to change it? Or, perhaps a more important question is whether we should try to change it. Are our political beliefs really worth fighting over?

HOW AMERICANS VIEW THEIR GOVERNMENT

For years, many Americans have expressed dissatisfaction with their government. According to the Pew Research Center, public trust in our government remains low. Only 20 percent of the population trusts what is coming out of Washington. More than two-thirds of Americans are of the opinion that politicians run for office to serve their own personal interests.

On specific issues, today's administration gets high grades for responding to natural disasters (70 percent favorable) and protecting our country (68 percent). Low marks are given for strengthening our economy (37 percent compared to 57 percent in 2020). And 75 percent feel that the current administration has dropped the ball on immigration.

Of course, the President is not all-powerful. There are some things he can do and some things that are beyond the scope of his power. The President as head of state and commander-in-Chief, can approve treaties once they are approved by the Senate, he can sign as well as veto bills and represent the United States in talks with foreign governments. He enforces the laws passed by Congress and can act to protect our country in times of war and peace. What a President cannot do is make laws, declare wars or decide how federal money is to be spent; nor can he interpret laws or choose a cabinet member or Supreme Court justice without senate approval.

GOD'S VIEW OF POLITICS

This book is not written to pass judgment on anyone but hopefully, to help open people's eyes. My primary intention is to simply look at politics through the eyes of God.

The first thing we need to do is take a look at what the Bible says regarding God's thinking about politics. The book of Romans tells us that we are subject to those who are in places of authority over us. In the 13th chapter of this book the Apostle Paul writes, "Let everyone be subject to the governing authorities, for there is no authority except that which God has established. The authorities that exist have been established by God. Consequently, whoever rebels against the authority is rebelling against what God has instituted, and those who do so will bring judgment on themselves" (Romans 13:1-2).

Who exactly were the governmental authorities that Paul was telling the early Christians to be obedient to? They certainly weren't good guys by any stretch of the imagination. The emperor was a fellow by the name of Nero Claudius Caesar Augustus Germanicus, better known simply as Nero. He was the fifth and final Caesar and arguably the worst. History remembers him as the emperor who "fiddled while Rome burned." After that catastrophic fire, he blamed it on Christians without any evidence to support this claim. He is said to have burned hundreds of Christians at the stake for their supposed involvement in this crime and even used some of them as human torches to light up the grounds of his palace during parties. He also reportedly murdered his mother, his wife and his step-brother in order to hold on to authority.

What about the local authorities? Judea, the province where Jesus was born lived and died, was under the rule of a succession of Herods during this time. In fact, there were so many Herods during the first century after Jesus' death and resurrection that it's almost impossible to tell them apart. The Bible usually doesn't explain which of the Herods it's talking about, but doesn't have much good to say about any of them. Let's take a look at some of what the Bible has to say about these "not-so-great" men:

> "When Herod realized that he had been outwitted by the Magi, he was furious, and he gave orders to kill all the boys in Bethlehem and its vicinity who were two years old and under..." (Matthew 2:16)

> "Now Herod had arrested John and bound him and put him in prison because of Herodias, his brother Philip's wife, for John had been saying to him: 'It is not lawful for you to have her.' Herod wanted to kill John, but he was afraid of the people, because they considered John a prophet. On Herod's birthday the daughter of Herodias danced for the guests and pleased Herod so much that he promised with an oath to give her whatever she asked. Prompted by her mother, she said, 'Give me here on a platter the head of John the Baptist.' The king was distressed, but because of his oaths and his dinner guests, he ordered that her request be granted and had John beheaded in the prison. (Matthew 14:3-12)

> "At that time some Pharisees came to Jesus and said to him, "Leave this place and go somewhere else. Herod wants to kill you." (Luke 13:31)

> "It was about this time that King Herod arrested some who belonged to the church, intending to persecute them. He had James, the brother of John, put to death with the sword. When he saw that this met with approval among the Jews, he proceeded to seize Peter also." (Acts 12:1-3)

Despite the cruelty of men like Nero and the Herods, Paul insists that Christians are subject to the governing authorities. Paul also says that God wants us to live quietly and to take care of our own affairs.

In 1 Thessalonians 4:11-12, he adds that that we are to walk properly before outsiders and depend solely on God. He wants us to know that God is in charge of our universe and that nothing ever happens by chance.

A TIME OF PERPETUAL ELECTIONS

As I write these words to you, the United States is just coming out of an election. What's more, we are about to go into another election. I recently read the words of a wise man who wrote that most people are almost always going into a storm, coming out of a storm or in the midst of a storm. I am totally in agreement with his statement. And I have come to believe that it applies to elections as well. We are either going into an election, coming out of an election or in the middle of an election.

Elections are necessary and I'm thankful that we have them. They provide all U.S. citizens with an opportunity to have their voices heard with regard to how our country is run. But there is one thing about elections that I absolutely hate! Can you guess what I'm talking about?

That's right! Political commercials on TV and Radio.

You just can't get away from them and it seems to me that most of them are full of lies and I cannot tolerate lies.

In my first book, entitled *Who Would Jesus Vote For?* I mentioned the differences between Democrats and Republicans. Certainly, when both parties began there were not many differences. However, there were some major issues like slavery. In the early years, Democrats stood for individual rights and state sovereignty and opposed national banks. They also opposed the abolition of slavery. It was the Republican Party, led by men like Abraham Lincoln, who opposed slavery on the basis that it was abhorrent and inhumane.

It was in 1932 that Franklin D Roosevelt revised the Democratic Party with the liberal policies of his New Deal Coalition. This coalition actually paved the way for Democrats to win every presidential election from 1932 to 1960. The only exception was Dwight Eisenhower, the heroic World War II general who was elected in 1952 and 1956. Eisenhower was actually pursued by both major parties before choosing to run as a Republican.

In recent years the Democratic Party has moved further to the left, supporting rights for gays, lesbians and transgender individuals. The Democratic Party is forcing the ideas of universal voting, social benefits for non-citizens and upholds religious secularism. In other words, the moral compass God gave to mankind has been shattered and discarded by the New Democrats.

The Democrats are focused on building a paradise on earth, where all people live in harmony and no one is judged because of their lifestyle or moral behavior. They want to erase the long-established boundaries of right and wrong and make it okay for men to marry men, women to marry women and where everyone is free to behave as he or she desires. They are following in the footsteps of others who have tried and failed to build utopian societies, but they have forgotten a couple of important truths:

1. No version of society that rejects God's laws will be able to stand for long.

2. "Unless the Lord builds the house, the builders labor in vain" (Psalm 127:1). What I mean by this is that any effort to build a paradise here on earth, without God's involvement, is doomed to failure. Paradise already exists. It is called "heaven" and it was built for those who love God and have chosen to accept Him as Lord and live in obedience to His commandments. Every attempt to build a man-made paradise on earth is doomed to failure.

Consider the hellish regimes that resulted from the Communist Party's attempts to build a paradise here on earth.

Unfortunately, all human beings are inherently corrupt. The Bible says that we are all sinners who have fallen short of the glory of God (Romans 3:23). We are tainted by sin and thus, everything we try to build on our own is also tainted by sin. Because of this it is bound to fail.

Is there anything we can do to help reverse the course of a world that seems headed for disaster and destruction? Please, keep reading.

CHAPTER TWO

WHO WOULD DEMONS VOTE FOR?

Demonic spirits have been living on this earth since the day Adam and Eve fell from grace, many thousands of years ago. They never grow tired of stirring up hatred between different races and people groups.

War? They love it.

Disease? One of their favorite means of inflicting pain and sorrow.

Poverty? It thrills them to see parents struggling to feed, clothe and otherwise provide for their children.

But more than anything else, they love it when they can get people to disobey God, to turn their backs on Him and live in sin.

Demons have long been involved in politics. Movements like Communism, Nazism and Fascism have come straight from the pit of hell. I believe that demons have been responsible for installing monstrous men into leadership positions around the world, killers like Josef Stalin, Mao Tse-Tung, Pol Pot, Idi Amin, Robert Mugabe and many more. In our day they are doing everything within their power to get us to put men and women in power who give no thought to God or His laws.

At this point you may be saying, "Demon spirits? Really!"

Yes, really!

Since sin entered the world fallen angels, better known as demons, have been involved in most areas where men are in charge especially with regard to the leadership of countries and political parties. Obviously, demons wanted to destroy human beings anyway they could. They still do. Their purpose is to get men and women into hell.

In his best-selling book, "The Return of the Gods," Messianic Rabbi and New York Times best-selling author Jonathan Cahn writes that "the gods (demons) were everywhere" in the ancient world. "For most of recorded time the gods were in every land and enthroned on the pinnacle of every major culture and civilization, from the god Enlil of Sumer (Sumer is the earliest known civilization in the history of Mesopotamia, emerging during the Chalcolithic and early Bronze Age) to Ra of Egypt, Dionysus of Greece, Peru of Russia, Juno of Rome, Shiva of India and a countless multitude of others."[1]

In other words, wherever there were people there were gods. These demon gods reigned over every nation, every city, every culture, in essence demons permeated the lives of everyone.   The Bible book of Deuteronomy tells us that people left God and turned to false gods. These other gods were known as Shedim, a word which first appears in Deuteronomy 32:17 (NASB). "They sacrificed to demons who were not God, to gods they have not known, New gods who came lately, whom your fathers did not dread." Shedim comes from the Hebrew root word "Shud" and means to act violently; to lay waste. In ancient Babylonian writings the word Shedim speaks of spirits. Reviewing Rabbi Cahn's book again we read, "When the ancient Jewish scholars rendered the Hebrew Bible into Greek, in a translation known as the Septuagint, they had to find the right word in Greek to stand for Shedim. The word they used could refer to a spirit, a principality, an occult entity, a god. The word was daimonion. It is from this that we get the word demon, a malevolent or evil being.

---

[1]   Cahn, Jonathan, "The Return of the Gods," (Frontline: Chicago) 2022

Although the Israelites were instructed not to have anything to do with the pagan nations or their gods, many of them began mixing worship of these demon-gods into the worship of Yahweh, the Creator of heaven and earth. They were doing satin's bidding, which essentially trampled what God wanted for their lives.

As Psalm 106:36-37 (NASB) says:

> "They served their idols, which became a snare for them. They even sacrificed their sons and daughters to the demons."

The takeaway for us is that the Jews forgot all the beautiful works the Lord had accomplished and decided to go it alone. They all lusted after physical comforts and material blessings and became disinterested in spiritual matters. They no longer cared about God or the commands he had given them. Instead, they cared about the things they saw that could give them a comfortable lifestyle. They were only interested in what they could see, what could they eat and what clothes and jewels they could wear.

My point in sharing this is simply to reveal the truth as to who and what is influencing your thinking. God makes it very clear in Ephesians 6:12:

> "For our struggle is not against flesh and blood, but against the rulers, against the powers, against the world forces of this darkness, against the spiritual forces of this darkness in the heavenly places."

CALLED TO SUBMIT

Our role is to obey God, to follow his leading and to "submit" to the authorities He has placed in power.

The key to understanding this scripture is to understand the word "submit." Romans 13:1 says that we are to submit to the governing bodies. 1 Peter 2:13 repeats the statement that we are to submit ourselves. In essence, submit means "to arrange things in an orderly fashion." God has concern for order and respect. That's why the Bible says in Luke 14:40, "Let everything be done in a fitting and orderly way."

According to the late historian/philosopher Howard Zinn, the main point for both Paul and Peter was their belief that governing authorities are necessary for keeping the peace.[2] Zinn goes on to say that slavery was lawful, the Holocaust was legal, as was segregation because the laws that allowed them were put in place to protect businesses rather than human beings. Therefore, when a Christian feels that his faith compels him to break an unjust law he should also be willing to submit to the lawful consequences. In instances where followers of Jesus are requested to do something sinful, they must refuse on the basis that their faith will not allow them to do anything unholy.

WHY WOULD GOD CHOOSE A BAD LEADER?

As Christians, we know that nothing happens in this world that God doesn't allow. It's not always easy to understand His purposes, but we must trust Him in all things. Yes, it's true that Satan is at work in the world right now. The day has not yet arrived when the devil and all of his demons will be destroyed forever. Until that day comes, our ancient enemy has a great deal of freedom even though God could annihilate him with a single glance. Again, we don't know the reason why God allows the devil to do so many horrible things but we know that it will all be made right someday.

Because of the way things are today, we can't say with certainty that every person who has been elected to high office is God's choice for the job. In some instances, these men and women may not be chosen because they are righteous God-fearing individuals, but rather because they have been chosen to inflict punishment on us for our ungodly behavior.

---

[2] Zinn, Howard, "A People's History of the United States (Harper, New York) 2017.

If you doubt that this is true, I urge you to take a quick look at the Old Testament books of I and II Kings and I and II Chronicles. In these books, you'll read about many of the kings that ruled over ancient Israel and Judah. Many of them were heroes of faith, who sought God in everything they did. But others were vicious tyrants who encouraged their people to worship false gods like the horrible Molek, who required child sacrifices, imprisoned and killed God's prophets and did many other horrible things.

Even some of the best kings of that day fell into great sin. David, who is described as "a man after God's own heart," (1 Samuel 13:14) murdered a man so he could have his wife. Solomon married hundreds of pagan women and became ensnared in the worship of idols.

There are many lessons to be learned through these Scriptures and one of these is that we can never put our complete faith in men (or women) because they will let us down. God is the only One who is completely steadfast and whose promises never fail. We cannot put our faith completely in any political party and that includes the Republicans, the Democrats, the Green Party or any other system developed by mankind. None of them are infallible, although it's clear that the platforms of some of these parties are more closely aligned with God's Word and His will. For example, the Democratic Party supports abortion a horrendous practice that most Christians could never approve. However, there are some Republicans who say they are "pro-choice" and there are undoubtedly some Democrats who oppose abortion (although I admit I can't think of any). My point is that we can't always trust in the label a politician wears.

Every believer should seek God's will and vote as He directs.

LET GOD'S WORD LEAD YOU

We must also read and meditate on God's Word so we will have a better understanding of His will.

Good God-fearing Christians can vote either way on many political issues. But not all of them.

- For example, God says "thou shalt not kill." How then could a Christian vote for someone who believes it's okay to kill unborn children?

- God also says that marriage is to be between one man and one woman. For that reason, I believe that no Christian could vote for the legalization of same-sex marriage, something that is totally against the teachings of Scripture.

- The Bible tells us that if a man refuses to work, he should not eat and yet we have a welfare system that squanders millions of dollars on able-bodied people who are not working only because they don't want to. (Admittedly we have to be very careful here. When Jesus was here on earth in the flesh He demonstrated great compassion for the poor, sick and those who were suffering in other ways. We must help those who are legitimately poor or disabled but we can't throw money at those who want to spend it on drugs or booze.).

CHAPTER THREE

BATTLE AT THE CAPITOL: WHO IS TO BLAME?

According to the Pew Research Center, the January 6, 2022 incident at the U.S Capitol was a flashpoint for most Americans. The only issue that both parties agreed on was that violence is never appropriate.

This was not the first time in American history that a person who was declared the loser in an election insisted that he had been cheated and that he was actually the rightful winner. But as far as I can find, this marked the first time these charges of fraud led to an assault on the capitol.

In the 2020 election, many Republicans believed there was widespread fraud. As I write this, more than two years after the votes were counted nearly two-thirds of Republicans still believe that Donald Trump was the rightful winner.

This is due not only to their admiration for Donald Trump, but because Republicans feel that we are living in an age riddled by scandal where propaganda has taken the place of unbiased news and it's difficult to know who to trust.

Journalist Anya van Wagtendonk wrote on January 21, 2022 that "almost half of Americans tell pollsters that they don't believe President Joe Biden Legitimately won the 2020 election. This is the "Big Lie" that inspired rioters to attempt to block the certification of the presidential election last January and remains at the center of the democratic emergency in the United States."[3] The rest of the story will play out in the near future. You can feel it coming as the "new far left" aims to revive socialism in the United States.

Larry Arnn, President of Hillsdale College, says that during the COVID pandemic support for socialism among the 16- to 23-year-old group jumped to 49 percent and socialism increased in popularity among all ages.

How did this happen? Corporate socialists saw their dreams coming to life. Government measures, introduced ostensibly to protect us from COVID destroyed businesses and eliminated competitors. It's our fault for not educating our youth as to the very real dangers of life under socialism.

It's time to make known the words of Winston Churchill:

> "Socialism is the philosophy of failure, the creed of ignorance, and the gospel of envy."[4]

A WORLD ON THE BRINK

Just look what's going on in the world around us. Russia announced they are annexing the Ukraine and their bombs and missiles have unleashed terror into residential neighborhoods and killed hundreds of innocent civilians, including many children. Vladimir Putin has even said that he would use nuclear weapons if Russia is provoked, putting the world closer to World War III than at any time since the Cuban Missile Crisis. There are many other conflicts around the world that have left millions of people dead. Since 1964, fighting in the Colombian conflict has taken over 220,000 lives. Then we have

---

[3] Anya van Wagtendonk," The Donald Trump's Big Lie that the 2020 election was stolen and its lasting damage to American democracy," The Messenger, January 21, 2022.

[4] Churchill, Winston, from a speech given at Perth Scotland on May 28, 1948

the Somali Civil War, conflicts in Nigeria, war in Sudan and South Sudan, etc.

Why is all of this happening?

You just read the reason. Fallen angels (demons) have been doing everything they can to influence our thinking, make us hate people who are different from us in any way especially with regard to their political thinking.

We must remember that our battle is not against a physical enemy but rather, against *"powers and principalities of darkness in the Heavenly places."*

In Ephesians 6:12, the Bible seems to identify a pecking order of demons all of whom do Satan's bidding.

> "For our struggle is not against flesh and blood, but against the rulers, against the authorities, against the powers of this dark world and against the spiritual forces of evil in the heavenly realms." (NIV)

The Bible refers to Satan as "the prince of this world" (John 12:31). Most of the people who share this planet with us are blinded by what the world offers. The Bible says, in 2 Corinthians 4:4, "in their case the god of this world has blinded the minds of the unbelievers, to keep them from seeing the light of the gospel of the Glory of Christ, who is the image of God," (ESV).

The purpose of the above information is to help us all understand that all the decisions we make, including political choices, are influenced by our beliefs. If you believe in God or better yet, if you trust in what God did through Jesus then everything you do will be shaped by your faith.

If you don't believe in God or His Son, I have one question for you: what will happen to you when you die?

Many people believe that they will go back to nothingness, that what they experience after death will be exactly like what they experienced before they were born. In other words, nothing at all.

But even those who claim to find comfort in this belief are susceptible to the fear of death that is common to all humankind. The Bible recognizes man's fear of death. In Job 18:14 (NASB) we read, "He is torn from the security of his tent, and they march him before the king of terrors."

Job goes to his tent; nothing is his and brimstone is scattered on his habitation. Memory of him perishes from the earth and he is driven from the light into the darkness. This will be the fate of those who don't believe.

OTHER REASONS FOR THE CHOICES WE MAKE

Although our faith or lack of faith is a major reason why we make the choices we do, there are numerous other factors. You may be influenced by the fact that you are a blue-collar worker, a first-time voter, an immigrant, a PhD in Economics, a priest, a professional athlete, etc.

The way you vote may also be influenced by your gender, your age, socio-economic status, level of education, ethnic background and so on.

No matter what their background may be, most people vote on which issues are most important to them and how those issues will impact their families. For example, the elderly look for security while the young look to reduce their costs.

People also choose to vote based on what they think of the incumbent or in the case of a presidential election, the current administration. If you aren't happy with the policies of the present administration, then it may be time to vote for a change. Perhaps you don't like our current economic situation or feel that we are spending too much money to help people in other nations and not enough to help people here at home. Other issues include abortion, immigration, immunizations, Critical Race Theory, whether the government should provide special support for transgender people, etc.

If you are a Democrat you want to expand social programs, encourage labor unions, expand regulations especially in the workplace, promote racial and gender equality, increase disability rights, advocate for an increase in regulations against environmental pollution and of course promote reform in our criminal justice system.

If you are a Republican, you are most likely opposed to abortion, seeing it as murder of unborn children. You most likely want to see our border security tightened, because you believe that the flood of immigrants into this country threatens our economy and opens us to threats from deadly drugs like fentanyl, the bloodthirsty cartels that sell them and other terrorists. You are likely to believe that labor unions have become too strong and powerful and that no government money should be spent to help people transition from one gender to the other and especially children.

As for issues such as Critical Race Theory which stresses the role of racism in the founding and growth of our country, Democrats say it must be taught because it presents a real issue that continues to play a huge part in our country today; whereas, Republicans feel that it exaggerates our country's flaws and only serves to foster hatred for the United States. They believe we should focus on the amazing possibilities that lie before us, instead of concentrating on the mistakes and tragedies of the past.

This is only a brief overview of a few of the issues that separate Democrats from Republicans. Most of these issues are extremely complex and it is not my purpose to go into them in detail.

Here's an important question I'd like us to consider:

Can we trust our elected officials to carry out the will of the people?

The answer is absolutely not!

Many politicians get rich off of land deals, stock tips and fill their pockets in many other dishonest ways. It's called cronyism! If you want to read more about the shenanigans that are enriching politicians on all points of the political spectrum, I urge you to read Peter Schweitzer's book *Throw them all out.*

The point I'm making here is that every thinking person has certain beliefs, convictions and a limit to what they will tolerate. You listen to the evening news after a hard day's work and wonder why things are the way they are in the world. You wonder why Vladimir Putin is killing so many innocents and what the United States, the strongest power in the world, is doing about stopping this war that could easily ramp up into World War III. You then think about what you would do if you were the person in charge. Egos have driven this war and Ukraine President Volodomyr Zelenskyy is no exception. His hard-line stance is behind many a child's death. And Putin is totally bullying a small, under-sized nation. Why? Because he thinks he will be the "person" to re-unite the old Russian Union and perhaps direct the entire world. And he doesn't seem to care how many lives it costs.

The question before us is, how do we find and choose trustworthy and honest leaders? The majority of people would say they want the people they vote for to be men and women of integrity. Unfortunately, given the incentives this world offers finding such individuals is not an easy task. Based on eighty years on this earth I believe that honest, trustworthy politicians are rare! There is almost always baggage of some kind. Remember the mythical character Diogenes, who went about with a lantern searching for an honest man? I urge you to be like him when it comes to selecting the men and women you will vote for. Remember these truths from the book of Proverbs:

"The integrity of the upright guides them, but the unfaithful are destroyed by their duplicity" (Proverbs 11:3), and "Whoever walks in integrity walks securely, but whoever takes crooked paths will be found out" (Proverbs 10:9).

Dishonesty is always discovered. It is like a house built upon sand which collapses when the waves and wind beat against it.

WHAT DO WE NEED IN A PRESIDENT?

As you prepare yourself to vote in the upcoming presidential election you may be wondering, what else do we need to look for in a President in addition to honesty. The answer is that we need a President who will work to protect the American people. He or she must be capable of leading our country to enjoy peace as we pursue prosperity. Our leader must be prepared to defend these first two issues by not being influenced by or aligned with groups of individuals who want rights that God would not allow. God gave man wisdom and our leaders must understand that wisdom is the application of Truth! My dad would always tell us that you can learn much about a person simply by seeing who he or she hangs out with. Or as the apostle Paul puts it in 1 Corinthians 15:33, "do not be misled: bad company corrupts good character."

Keep in mind what you read a few minutes ago: "For our struggle is not against flesh and blood, but against the rulers, against the powers, against the world forces of this darkness, against the spiritual forces of wickedness in the heavenly places."

A CLOSER LOOK AT OUR TWO PARTIES

Because I want you to understand what the Democratic and Republican parties believe, I urge you to look through their platforms for yourself and see which one better fits your beliefs. You can download pdfs of the two platforms online. They are long (around 100 pages of small text) and complex in some areas, but well worth reviewing. The platforms cover issues like immigration, taxation, abortion, same sex marriage and much more. Just be sure that you are reading the most recent platforms, as they are amended in every Presidential election year.

Keep in mind that you can only live and vote on what you believe!

In other words, your vote for a Democrat or Republican is also a vote for the Democratic or Republican platform. For example, if you say you vote Democratic but are not in favor of abortion, then you are not a Democrat. This is a very important point. Suppose you are a Catholic but vote for a Democratic candidate for Senate knowing full well this person's beliefs are opposed to the church's teaching that abortion is murder. How can you square your vote with your faith? The answer is, you can't.

This dilemma has no compromise. You are either pregnant or you are not pregnant. You can't be "a little bit pregnant." This is true even though the U.S Catholic Bishops gave an ambiguous answer to the question of a Catholic voting for a pro-abortion candidate. "This is a decision to be made by each Catholic, guided by a conscience formed by Catholic moral teaching." In other words, "It's your decision!" What does that tell you? God says, "Thou shall not kill," (Exodus 20:13, KJV) and who are we to trifle with this commandment? The church should be much more assertive on this issue.

The Bible is very clear on the fact that God created human life and He decides when you die. If you are a truly born-again Christian, then surely you will support a pro-life platform. Why

would anyone want to kill a baby in the womb? There is no logical reason, only selfish interests.

And the doctors who perform these killings are essentially murderers!!

God is not fooling around when He tells us "Choose life in order that you may live" (Deuteronomy 30:19, NIV).

CHAPTR FOUR

WHO ARE YOU AND WHERE ARE YOU HEADED?

Choosing life means to pick the lifestyle God meant for you. Death (the pleasure road) has a certain allure, a certain "pick this fruit and you will be like God" attitude. Those who follow this road may indulge in excessive alcohol consumption, indiscriminate sex, drugs, etc. But those who do try to find pleasure in such endeavors soon find that these temporary thrills quickly evaporate. They turn on us and bring heartache and destruction instead of joy.

Surely if given a do-over, Freddie Mercury the late front man of the band Queen would rethink his excessive lifestyle. Extremely talented, loved by many, his choices were self-destructive. Choosing life means choosing what God has done to get you sanctified. It means to avoid lifestyles that promote deviant sex, avoid all religions that promote pleasure. Choosing life is not wasting the talents God blessed you with. We are to avoid the dangers of pornography and to stop committing slow suicide by wasting time in front of a TV or simply eating like a pig.

Elvis Presley is another who had everything a man could possibly want. Fame, adoring fans, millions of dollars, a beautiful mansion to call home. He could have enjoyed a long life of luxury but instead he died at the relatively young age of 42, a bloated caricature of what he should have been. Why? Because he lost sight of the things that are truly valuable in life and indulged himself in pleasures of the flesh.

And these are only two examples of hundreds of men and women who have unwittingly chosen death over life.

DON'T TAKE THE EASY WAY OUT

In life, we are often faced with difficult choices to make but we must not take the easy way out. When it comes to politics, we can't always vote for the candidate or party that promises us an easy time of it. When we are voting it's important to ask, "how will this impact me?" But it's even more important to ask, "how will this impact my community or my country?"

For example, everyone wants lower taxes. Show me a man who says, "I'd really like to see my taxes go up," and I'll show you a man who needs a few sessions with a good psychiatrist. And yet, it may be a mistake to vote for someone who promises to whittle our taxes down to next to nothing.

Don't get me wrong. I generally hate the idea of paying taxes. As a business owner, I've certainly paid more than my share. If I could meet the man who invented taxes, I'd probably punch him in the nose. Nor am I in agreement with the idea that people who make more money should pay higher taxes. This seems to me to be a tax on innovation and creativity and I believe it stifles both. But I also understand that we must have a system in place to help pay for the upkeep of our roads, bridges, and the rest of our infrastructure (The operative word here is "necessary.").

My point in all of this is that we must be willing to look beyond our own self-interests when we cast our ballots. As John F. Kennedy said in his inaugural speech, "ask not what your country can do for you, but what you can do for your country."

THE NEED FOR "MEANING"

Victor Frankl, a renowned psychologist and philosopher was imprisoned by the Nazis in World War II. In the midst of terrible suffering, humiliation and unbelievable brutality, he discovered that man's most important and strongest drive was not his will for pleasure or for power but rather, his desire to find meaning!

Helping others was far more important than anything else. According to Frankl, as people came into the concentration camps they experienced extreme shock as they realized they were being held captive by a madman. After a period of time, these same people became very apathetic. This occurred as they became accustomed to daily life and camp existence. But in the midst of their apathy, they all helped each other, doing what they could to make sure that everyone survived.

Frankl concluded that the meaning of life is found in every moment of being alive. He also concluded that "prisoner's psychological reactions are not solely the result of conditions of life, but also from the freedom of choice he always has, even during severe suffering. Every person, including a prisoner in the worst jail, has to have hope in the future. Once he or she loses that hope, he is doomed."[5]

One of the greatest rights that any citizen of the United States can have is the right to vote. Ask yourself how would your Heavenly Father direct you to vote? Does your vote benefit others or does it cause unnecessary burdens to be placed upon them? In other words, is your vote a reflection of the meaning you ascribe to your life? Does it match up with your understanding of why God created you? If not, it's time to reconsider some of your choices.

---

[5]   Frankl, Victor E, "Man's Search for Meaning," (Beacon Press, Boston) Published in the United States in 1959.

OUR FREEDOMS ARE BEING ERODED

I believe that abortion is an extremely serious issue that breaks the heart of God. But there are many other issues that require our immediate attention. For example, we are rapidly losing our freedoms to a government that seems to be following in the footsteps of George Orwell's alarming and classic book, *1984.*

We live in the most prosperous country in the world but I am afraid it is changing! Big Brother has the ability to eavesdrop on most cell phone conversations. Other countries hate us and want us eradicated all because of the blessings God has poured out on us, primarily for always being on the side of the Israelis His chosen people.

Consider the following: the FBI and the NSA (National Security Agency) keep dossiers on most American citizens. Electronic records are recorded on every credit card purchase you make. Telephone companies also keep detailed records on your phones, faxes, texts and emails. And now, with Alexa and Siri, your most intimate actions and personal comments are recorded. Google tracks every site you visit and your cars are equipped with a GPS device that monitors your every move.

If that's not scary enough, cameras are literally everywhere, in buildings, on highways and streets, in parking lots. They are all over. As crazy as it seems, there are many political party executives who are proponents of "chipping" everyone, which sounds like something right out of the book of Revelation.

I could go on and on but you get the picture.

Another question that arises is "can elections be rigged?" Based on the above, certainly. If you have enough money, you can impose your will on the American people. All this is leading to a modified dictatorship. You may be saying to yourself that this could never happen, there are too many checks and balances!

But you would be wrong. Based on what we have witnessed these past few years, the question is "could the USA evolve into a Fascist state?" In other words, a "totalitarian country?" Far-fetched, you say? Not really.

Just look at the way our government has been imposing more and more regulations and stripping away more and more freedoms every year. We are no longer a nation of character, but a nation in debt. We are no longer the world's most powerful nation, but something much less. Our national focus has been drawn away from keeping our military strong, our people fed and restoring self- respect so that bail-outs and stimulus checks are no longer necessary. Instead of trying to keep our country strong and free, we have spent our energy coming up with a set of "rights" for every form of sexual perversion.

Totalitarian in its simplest meaning is that there is a central ruler that controls all aspects of your life by any means necessary. Personal freedoms are not considered.

This form began thousands of years ago with a biblical character named Nimrod, whose great ambition was to rule the world. I personally can't think of anything quite as frightening as the idea of a one-world government. Only God has the right and power to rule the world and as we know from recent history, man is not God. The Communists sought to usher in a world-wide Utopia but brought decades of mass pain and sorrow instead murdering many millions of people in countries like Russia, China and Cambodia.

CHAPTER FIVE

THE PUSH FOR A ONE-WORLD GOVERNMENT

The communists are not the only ones who dream of a one-world government. Many liberals and leftists long for the same thing. They believe that such a government will usher in world peace by eliminating nationalism, establishing one currency to be used by all humankind and by bringing about a level playing field where there are no super-rich countries or super-poor countries.

The problem is that these dreamers have not taken human nature into consideration. I believe what the Bible says when it tells us that we are all sinners, creatures who fall short of the glory of God. We are natural-born liars and cheaters who struggle to do what's right until we have surrendered ourselves to the grace offered by Jesus Christ. I also believe that Satan exists and that he will do anything within his power to destroy us.

Erasing national boundaries will not do anything to eliminate racism or animosity toward other ethnic groups. For example, after centuries of hatred will Pakistanis and Indians suddenly get along because they are now under the same government? Will Russians and Ukrainians throw down their arms and embrace each other? I don't think so.

But the worst thing about a one-world government is that it would open the door to a world dictator. Can you imagine the devastation that would take place if a monster in the mold of Adolf Hitler were to take control of such a government? Or a psychopath like Josef Stalin?

Anyone who doesn't think it would happen obviously doesn't know very much about human nature. History is filled with accounts of horrible leaders who inflicted great pain on their subjects. I'm talking about Roman Emperors like Nero and Caligula, who murdered their own family members to retain power and slaughtered their own subjects. Read through the Old Testament and you will see that many of the kings of ancient Israel and Judah were evil. Then there were men like Genghis Kahn, Attila the Hun and Ivan the Terrible, each of whom were responsible for many thousands of deaths often brought about by the most cruel and horrible means possible. And in modern times we have seen the unbelievable cruelty of men like Adolf Hitler, Joseph Stalin, Mao Zedong, Idi Amin, Pol Pot and many others.

What strikes me is that some of the worst dictators of modern times started out as reformers, people who wanted to eradicate poverty in their countries and help their people. But as time went on, they proved the truth of the old adage that "power corrupts and absolute power corrupts absolutely."

Consider Robert Mugabe, who ruled in Zimbabwe (formerly Rhodesia) for 37 years. He started out as a statesman who sought to establish economic reforms, eliminate poverty and bring about racial reconciliation. But by the end of his life, he had become a bloodthirsty dictator whose main goal seemed to be to hang on to power. In order to do this, he put thousands of people in jail and killed thousands more.

When I look at what the leaders of "one-country governments" have done in terms of stirring up trouble and strife, it makes me determined to do everything I can to make sure that a one-world government never happens. How about you? Will you join with me in voting against the rising tide of globalists who are unwittingly leading us toward danger. When I was a student at Georgetown University in the school of business, we were blessed to have a history professor named Carroll Quigley, PhD. He taught on the development of civilizations. I mention this because several of his books identified a plan for a one-world government. He taught that the future can be better than the past and that each of us has a moral responsibility to make it happen.

It is safe to say that the occult is behind this push for a one world government. In 1918 Cecil Rhodes (and his occult- driven secret society) ceded control to J.P. Morgan (who was deeply involved in astrology and the occult) and his American group called The Council on Foreign Relations. Their main objective was to establish a one-world government with a world financial system and a one-world religion.

IT ALL STARTED WITH NIMROD

Nimrod a character mentioned four times in the Bible, seems to be the first person to try to establish a one-world government. The Bible doesn't tell us much about him, merely that he was a mighty hunter and warrior and that he was the son of Cush who was the grandson of Abraham.

But we can learn much more about him from extra-biblical sources. For example, Nimrod was apparently a great king and the first ruler to wear a crown to signify his authority. He is said to have introduced fire worship and idolatry, then received instruction in divination for three years from Bouniter the fourth son of Noah.

According to the *Encyclopedia Britannica*, an early Arabic work (*Kitab al-Magall or "Book of Rolls"*) says that Nimrod reigned for 69 years. Nimrod is also mentioned in the Clementine Literature. One version of the Clementines (Recognitions R4:29) says that Nimrod was king in the land of Shinar (Mesopotamia) and was also the founder of Nineveh. In the Homilies (H 9:4-6) Nimrod is reported to be the same as Zoroaster.

Flavius Joseph, a Jewish Historian, mentioned that Nimrod was a man who set his will against God's. According to Flavius, Nimrod proclaimed himself as a god and both he and his wife Semiramis were worshipped as gods by their subjects.

According to other sources Nimrod lived some 200 years after the Great Flood destroyed all life on earth, with the exception of Noah and his family. Unfortunately, when Nimrod heard stories about the flood, he did not understand that the destruction was necessary due to man's evil behavior. Instead, he resented God and vowed that he would never let such a thing happen again.

According to this legend, Nimrod was the originator and overseer of the building of the great Tower of Babel (You may remember the story from the 11th chapter of Genesis.). The story of Nimrod says that one of the reasons for the building of the tower was to protect humankind from any further floods. If God decided to again destroy the world in this way, people would be able to climb to the top of the tower where the water could not reach them and be safe there.

Apparently, Nimrod did not want people to depend on God nor fear Him. Instead, he taught his subjects to depend upon their own strength and wisdom (Does this sound familiar? It should, because this is the basis of today's secular humanism.). This should not come as a surprise to us because Nimrod's name comes from the word "marad," which means "he rebelled." He also introduced idols to turn them away from the one true God and introduced the idea of communicating with and worshiping the dead.

You see this today in primitive tribes buried deep in the Amazon jungle. They try to communicate with their dead ancestors, hoping their ancient relatives can provide guidance regarding present problems and life after death. Instead of turning to the One who really has all the answers – that is, God himself – they turn to the dead, to witchcraft and necromancy, all of which are expressly forbidden by the Bible.

CHAPTER SIX
THE BIRTH OF THE OCCULT

The five major false religions of the ancient world all had a common denominator. Superstition! *Encyclopedia Britannica* defines this as an excessively credulous belief in and reverence for Supernatural Beings. These beliefs are passed on to the next generation and so Satan's lies are perpetuated and its tentacles spawn other lies. For example, after Nimrod's death, his widow Semiramis promoted his deification thus ensuring her continued praises as queen of the earth. She is credited with masterminding the "secret religion of Babylon." Mythology has Semiramis ascending to heaven as a dove, where she would be known as Inanna the fertility goddess.

Ralph Woodrow writes in his book *Babylon Mystery Religion,* that "Babylon is the source of false religion."[6] Woodrow traces the practices and teachings of ancient Babylon and their modern counterparts in the Roman Catholic Church and her Protestant daughters. Sadly, much of Christianity is permeated with false doctrines from Babylon.

The story of Nimrod and Semiramis could be described as "the birth of the occult." Nimrod's followers gave him many names: he became the Roman god Bacchus (which means son of Cush the god of wine and revelry). He was also known as Marduk, Kronos (the horned one) and Saturn. The Phoenicians and the Rhodesians annually sacrificed their children to Kronos.

---

[6] Woodrow, Ralph, "Babylon Mystery Religion," (Ralph Woodrow Evangelistic Association; Palm, Springs, CA) 1981

To some, he was known as Ninus (the son). Others called him Zoroaster, (the seed of Aster). Keep in mind that Zoroaster through the ages was considered the promised seed. The Greeks referred to Nimrod as Dionysus (the sin bearer) and also gave him homage as Zeus (the savior) and Mithras (the mediator). The Babylonians worshipped Nimrod as El-Bar (god the son). It should be clear that there is one and only one "sin bearer, savior and mediator" and that is the Lord Jesus.

In some ancient civilizations, the name Nimrod is found in conjunction with snakes and dragons. As a matter of fact, Nimrod appropriated these devil-like icons as his personal emblems. Therein lies the development of associating Nimrod with Satan.

Fast forward to the Book of Revelation, where we read:

> "A great sign appeared in heaven, a woman clothed with the sun, and the moon under her feet and on her head a crown of twelve stars; and she was with Child... Then another sign appeared in heaven: and behold, a great red dragon having seven heads and ten horns. . . .and she gave birth to a son..." (Revelation 12:1-5, NASB)

The pregnant woman in this vision is God's chosen nation. The infant represents God's promised Savior (see Genesis 3:15). The woman in labor is Israel. The fearsome red dragon is the same red dragon portrayed with the sun god in the *Mystery Religion of Babylon*! His name is Satan.

Starting with Herod's attempt to kill all the male infants in Bethlehem, to the crucifixion of Yeshua (Jesus), all of Satan's attempts to thwart God's plans for humankind have failed. Satan has tried again and again to destroy the Jews because he knows that the Jewish people are so important to the carrying out of God's plans for our future. For example, it was the Jewish race through which the Messiah, Jesus Christ, came into the world. And the return of the Jewish people to Israel will help to pave the way for Christ's return to this earth. If Satan could destroy the Jewish people, he could thwart God's plans for the salvation of the people He created. But that will never happen!!!!!

Whether or not all these myths about Nimrod are correct is immaterial. As a result of these many legends most of mankind was drawn into worship of false gods and occult practices began to spread throughout the world, despite God's commands against them. As Deuteronomy 18:9-13, says, ". . .there shall not be found among you anyone who uses divination, one who practices witchcraft, or one who interprets omens, or a sorcerer, or one who casts a spell, or a medium, or a spiritist, or one who calls up the dead. For whoever does these things is detestable to the Lord."

What prompted man's interest in pursuing this avenue when God said not to? How did we get drawn into the darkness? Temptation is something all Christians struggle with on a daily basis. What makes people interested in things God said to avoid? Have you ever noticed that little children are often insistent on doing whatever it is their parents have told them not to do. Tell a child not to touch a hot stove, and it's almost certain that he'll head straight for it. Tell him to stay away from a mud puddle and suddenly that muddy mess will seem like the most wonderful attraction in all the world.

We human beings are born with a streak of rebellion and many of us never grow out of it. We are like Eve in the Garden of Eden. As soon as God told her to stay away from the forbidden fruit, it looked like the most delicious, beautiful, juicy thing she had ever laid eyes on. It looked irresistible to her and Satan was more than happy to help her get a few bites.

In addition to our natural tendency to rebel, some people get involved in the occult because they believe it will give them an advantage in some way.

Luke writes, in Acts 16:17, (NASB) "Now it happened, as we went to prayer, that a certain slave girl possessed with a spirit of divination met us, who brought her masters much by fortune telling. . ."

Today, the occult is still big business. We can see it in the prolif-eration of "psychic hotlines" and other such come-ons. Almost every community that is big enough to have a grocery store and a gas station also has a commercial psychic. Most of these people are self-promoting charlatans and tricksters, although there may be some who receive information from the dark side of the supernatural.

Some of these "gifted" psychics have become very rich through their books, television shows and other public appearances. They have become very well-respected despite the fact that when they try to tell the future, they are invariably wrong. For example, The National Enquirer annually runs an article featuring a number of top psychics' predictions for the upcoming year. Those predictions almost never have anything to do with reality. The cataclysmic events they predict don't happen. The earthquakes, fires and other major events that do occur are not mentioned in their predictions. You would think that such a performance would get them removed from the list of the world's top psychics, but it doesn't seem to do so.

Do we really want these people telling us how to vote? I don't think so but this is often what we get. People listen to these "psychics" and do what they say to do, even though they do not have one shred of accuracy. All men, from every age, want to know what is to come in the future.

That's why "prophets" like Nostradamus are so popular. As you may know, Nostradamus was a French astrologer born in 1503. He had sev-eral wives and seven children. He opened a medical practice in Agen during the 1530s and began his prophecies about 1547. He used the planets, the sun and the moon to predict the future. In many ways, he is the poster child for fortune telling. His prophecies are vague and extremely hard to understand. This lack of clarity makes it easy to apply them to different events that have happened over the centuries as in "well, he must be talking about World War II, and this part must refer to President Kennedy's assassination." The cleverness of Nostradamus seems to lie in the fact that he made his prophecies broad enough that they can be linked to many different occurrences and situations and not to the fact that he was so good at predicting. Admittedly, one of the things that makes Nostradamus hard to understand is that he wrote his prophecies over 500 years ago. It's a bit like trying to read Chaucer. Then again, his archaic language makes him sound mysterious and helps to convince many of his giftedness.

Here's what the Bible says about such fortune tellers:

"If a prophet or a dreamer arises among you and gives you a sign or a wonder, and the sign or wonder that he tells you comes to pass, and if he says 'let us go after other gods' which you have not known, 'let us serve them' <u>you shall not listen to the words</u>" (Deuteronomy 13:1-3, ESV), (emphasis mine).

Moses warned the people of Israel that there might arise among them workers of signs who would produce wonders or who would speak a word and it would come to pass but then they would speak against what God has already revealed in His Word. God will never tempt you, but He will test you. In other words, if you are enticed by a person who believes in witchcraft or the occult you must not listen to him or her. God allows this to find out if you truly love Him with all your soul. And conversely if you are enticed you can know that no matter what, God will not stop loving you or pursuing you for His kingdom. As a matter of fact, you literally have to fight God to go to hell.

In David Guzik's commentary, he states "Godly discernment examines the message of the spiritual leader." Experiences and wonders are often wrought by evil spirits. For example, the Church of Scientology claims that billions of extra-terrestrial beings were sent to earth by Xenu, dictator of the galactic confederacy. These alien souls then attached themselves to chosen humans known as Thetans, who one day will be saved from their spiritual darkness. Who could believe such an absurd story? Millions of people who are enticed by the occult and ready to listen to Satan's lies.

Keep in mind that every false religion, which includes anything associated with the occult, comes from the mind of man! What about the breakaway sects from mainstream religions. These groups go beyond traditional teachings into more esoteric practices. We just mentioned one, Scientology. Mysticism could possibly be the oldest as it was found in hunter-gatherer societies. In these religions, Shamans would slip into trances claiming to speak with the dead; they also claimed they were fighting against evil spirits. Most lived apart from the community and practiced self-discipline (Asceticism). Jewish mysticism (Kabbalah) first appeared in the 12th century. Next for the Jews came Hasidic Judaism, which began in the 1700's starting in Eastern Europe as a spiritual revival. Its founder was Baal Shem Tov (master of the good name) its teachings a mystical connection with God through study, prayer and dancing.

It is a tragedy that so many people have spent their entire lives searching for answers, but never finding them. This is because they look in all the wrong places, instead of turning to the One who is the Way, the Truth and the Life, the answer to all of our questions, Jesus Christ the Son of God.

In the Book "Magic and Witchcraft in the West" edited by David Collins, S.J. we read, "the transition from impurity to purity is one of the basic goals and regular elements of magic rituals in all ancient near eastern cultures. Near Eastern magic as a whole can be subdivided into four categories: Liminal Magic (Liminal occupying a position on both sides of a boundary "liminal space between past and present"), Defensive Magic (user possesses defensive skills that are enhanced by magical powers allowing them to have protective properties, e.g. aloe, black pepper etc.), Aggressive Magic (defined as the use of rituals and incantations for gaining advantage or control over another person) and Witchcraft: (the use of spells for evil purposes)."[7]

---

[7]   Collins, David J., S.J., "The Cambridge History of Magic and History in the West" (Cambridge University Press: Cambridge, England) 2018.

CHAPTER SEVEN

KNOW THE TIMES YOU LIVE IN

As I look around and see what is going on in the world today, I am convinced that we are living in the last days of planet earth. So much of what the Bible says will happen in the end times are happening right now!

End-time prophecies that are found in the Bible can be broken down into two categories; near events and at-the-door events. Near events would include the regathering of the Jews to Israel, the emergence of false prophets, an increase in knowledge, travel, lawlessness and moral decay and a major increase in occult activity.

The apostle Paul writes, "But the spirit explicitly says that in the latter times some will fall away from the faith, paying attention to deceitful spirits and doctrines of demons" (1 Timothy 4:1). Never in the history of the world has there been such a revival of astrology, witchcraft, etc.

In case you haven't noticed, occult practices are booming. For example, the Pew Research Center notes that witchcraft is surging. Millennials and celebrities have embraced it in a big way. Trinity College in Connecticut, conducted a survey in 1990 in which they found that there were about 8,000 members of Wicca in 1990. Today, there are over 300,000 Wiccans (witches) in the United States.

In 2018 Pew Research Center also found that many people who consider themselves to be Christians believe in things like reincarnation, astrology, psychics and that there is spiritual energy in physical objects like mountains and trees.

Such beliefs are known collectively as part of the "new age" movement. They are not found anywhere in the Bible and are in fact opposed to the teachings of Christ.

These new age ideas are really a mixture of many different beliefs, mostly rooted in Easter Mysticism.

The proliferation of these teachings reminds me what Paul wrote to Timothy: "For the time will come when they will not endure sound doctrine; but wanting to have their ears tickled, they will accumulate for themselves teachers in accordance to their own desires; and will turn away from the truth, and will turn aside to myths" (2 Timothy 4:3-4).

The Apostle was deeply concerned that once he was gone false teachers would spread lies that would cause the people to reject the truth. We see today that Paul's concerns were valid. We live in a world where what I call "buffet religion" is popular. People choose to believe what pleases them and reject what seems hard to them. They are like diners going through the line at a buffet, taking a little bit of this and a little bit of that. A big heaping of Hinduism, a dash of Buddhism and a couple of spoonfuls of Christianity. They think they can have their own truth, but it doesn't work that way. Easy and pleasurable are what most individuals want, so they search for preachers who tell part truths and all enjoy the sermons.

The problem with this is that "There is one body and one Spirit, just as also you were called in one hope of your calling; one Lord, one faith, one baptism, one God and Father of all who is over all and through all and in all" (Ephesians 4:4-6). And remember what Jesus said, "I am the way, and the truth, and the life; no one comes to the Father but through Me" (John 14:6).

Remember that old Burger King jingle, "have it your way?" Well, with all respect to Burger King, you can't always have it your way. You must take it God's way!

This is true in politics too. It would be nice to think that we can go easy on criminals because all people are basically good and when someone promises that they will behave we can always trust them. But it doesn't work that way.

It would be wonderful if we didn't have to worry about fraud in the welfare system because people are basically honest. But while there are many truly needy people who deserve a helping hand, there are also millions who are out to steal as much as they can get.

It would be terrific if we didn't have to spend so much money on weapons because we can trust other nations to tell us the truth at all times and never launch a surprise attack against us. But then we must remember what happened at Pearl Harbor.

My point is that life on this earth is not always the way we want it to be. When it comes to our politics, we have to vote with our eyes wide open seeing things the way they really are instead of the way we wish they were.

As an example of this, I think of what happened in this country back in the late 1960s and early 1970s, when many thousands of young people dropped out of what they considered to be a corrupt society that was badly in need of correction (yes, I'm talking about the hippies). These people wanted to go back to the land, work with their hands and grow their own food. They talked about peace, love and acceptance. They wanted a world where there was no such thing as war and everyone was free to do as he or she pleased.

Unfortunately, they didn't understand that war is sometimes inevitable in order for freedom to exist, that there are people like Adolf Hitler and Josef Stalin (and perhaps Vladimir Putin?) who must be opposed with military might. In striving to live free, they cast off all restraints including the laws of God. Nor did they understand that "freedom" doesn't give us the right to act in ways that hurt others.

What happened to the hippy movement? Its good intentions were quickly corrupted by rampant drug abuse, promiscuous sex, physical and mental laziness and confusion. These often-well-meaning people saw the world in a way that it never was and never could be. Over time, they became a laughingstock. Our politics must be grounded in reality.

AMERICA IN THE LAST DAYS

People sometimes ask me, "Where is the United States in the end-times scenario?" The answer is that America is not mentioned in any end-times discussions. Most prophecy preachers point to the fact that we are simply "one of the other nations" as mentioned in the book of Revelation. Revelation 18:3 comes to mind. From my perspective, especially after reviewing the mid-term elections of 2022, it seems to me that the United States has been removed from the leadership of this world only to be replaced by a much weaker counterfeit. God is long-suffering but He cannot be mocked. At some point He says, "enough is enough." America, if you want the wide pleasure road then you shall have it along with its consequences. If you want a platform of unbelievers, then so it will be.

For a complete review of the Last Days, please see my book "Yesterday, Today & Tomorrow." Within its pages you will find many facts pertinent to the end of this age, facts that I have only touched upon in this book.

Many signs of Christ's return are given in the scriptures. One very important sign is simply to look at sheep. In all domesticated animals there is a homing button that helps them return to their home shelter, all except sheep. They are the most helpless animals and will spend their day grazing and never look up. Consequently, they get lost. They have as mentioned, no homing instincts. Even if their sheepfold is directly in front of them and in plain sight, they will not find it on their own. The only way is to follow their shepherd.

The Bible tells us in John 10:7, "So Jesus said to them again, Truly, truly I say to you I am the door of the sheep." Notice that Jesus did not say that He is "a door," which by definition would imply that there are other doors. In the ninth verse of the same chapter, He says, "I am the door; if anyone enters through Me, he will be saved, and go in and out and find pasture." Once again, Christ is the one and only door.

By their very nature, sheep are followers and easily helpless against predators. When predators pursue the herd, they do not run but huddle up and thus are easy pickings. They are also easily prone to injury and if by chance a sheep is to fall into a moving stream, he or she will drown. Coincidentally, sheep will not drink from a stream of moving water. That is why Psalm 23:2 says that the Lord leads us by "still waters." Sheep will only drink from still water sources.

Can you see the comparison between sheep and men? Sheep are totally dependent upon the shepherd, who constantly cares for their flock. In the evenings when other flocks are present and the sheep co-mingle, only the voice of their shepherd will be able to move them. Now on occasion when the flock was in the open country, as evening approached, the shepherd would gather his flock. He would leave a small opening and then lay down across that opening, thus preventing any wild beasts from entering. Essentially the shepherd was laying down his life to protect his flock from both beasts and robbers. With Christ we are always loved, cared for and protected.

Another question I hear is, "when will Christ return?"

Here's what the Bible has to say about that: "But of that day and hour no one knows, not even the angels of heaven, nor the Son, but the Father alone. For the coming of the Son of Man will be just like the days of Noah. For as in those days they were eating and drinking, marrying and giving in marriage, until the day that Noah entered the Ark" (Matthew 24:36-37).

God is saying here is how to know when I am coming: look around and you'll see that it's exactly as it was in the **days of Noah!**

Other "at the door" signs include: The rebuilding of the temple in Jerusalem, earthquakes, all nations coming together against Israel, the mark of the beast, etc. All of the above are signs that the antichrist is about to be revealed to the world and he will unite religion, economics and politics.

He will be hailed as a great hero; the man the world has long waited for, the man who will unite us and enable us to work together to solve our problems. He will be idolized and worshiped by people throughout the world.

And then he will reveal his true colors.

The world will discover a ruthless monster underneath the benign mask. His goal will not be to assist humankind, but rather to enslave us and then destroy us.

How can we escape the death and destruction he has planned for us? The only way we can be saved is to surrender ourselves to God and trust Him to watch over us. God will protect and care for those who belong to Him.

The Bible doesn't tell us exactly how the antichrist will come to power, but I believe that he will most likely be elected to office by a landslide. So, first of all, we can be very careful in the choices we make. Ask God to help you be able to discern between what is true and what is a lie. If a politician is making promises that sound too good to be true, they probably are. Another thing we can do is to search the Scriptures to compare what any politician is saying with what God says in His Word. God's Word is like a mighty lighthouse that will stand forever, guiding men and women safely into the harbor of God's love. Anyone who disregards the light will wind up broken on the rocks that Satan has hidden along the shore. If anyone says anything that is in conflict with God's Word, we can be certain that he or she is wrong.

I would also say to beware of politicians who claim to be Christians, but who twist God's words to support their own particular philosophy. I have met many people who claimed to be Christians who actually believed they were Christians, but

their beliefs were tangled up with New Age teachings. They are particularly dangerous because they use half-truths to help spread their lies.

We must not be fooled.

SIGNS THAT THE LAST DAYS ARE NEAR

The following is a short summary of some of the signs from the Bible that show us that Christ's return is near:

> **There will be a proliferation of false prophets.** We have seen this in the rise of people like Jim Jones, David Koresh, Shoko Asahara, Marshall Applewhite, and others. Such false teachers eventually lead their followers to death.

> **The Nation of Israel will be restored.** This occurred in 1948, when a homeland for the Jewish people was established in the Middle East on land that was promised to Abraham and his descendants thousands of years ago.

> **There will be wars and rumors of wars.** As I write these words, there are 27 wars raging in various parts of the world. There have been over 800 wars in the world since historians began keeping count.

> **There will be major increases in lawlessness and moral decay.** All you have to do to see that this is happening is to read your morning newspaper or watch the evening news. Actually, I would recommend that you don't watch the news right before bedtime. If you do, you'll probably find it hard to sleep after seeing all the "lawlessness and moral decay" that is taking place all around us.

SIGNS THAT JESUS IS "AT THE DOOR."

Here is a brief summary of some of the Bible's signs that Jesus' return is imminent.

> **The Temple will be scheduled to be re-built in Jerusalem.** Plans are already being made for this. Keep your eye out for more important news from the Middle East.

> **All the nations of the world will hate Israel and stand against her.** Already, Israel has very few friends in the world. Although she is often required to defend herself against terrorists and missile attacks, she is accused of instigating the violence. The United States is one of the few countries in the world that supports Israel, but forces are at work that are trying to change this.

> **Earthquakes all over the world will increase in frequency and magnitude.** This is clearly happening.

> **A one-world government will force people to receive the mark of the beast on their bodies.** Those who refuse the mark will be unable to purchase food or other essentials. Unification of the world is inevitable. The book of Revelation tells us the anti-Christ will unite the world's political, religious and economic systems. This doesn't mean we shouldn't stand against this. We can't afford to just "give up" and say, "there's nothing I can do about it." After all, God hears and responds to the prayers of His people.

> **Occult activity will grow rapidly.** A word of warning to those who consider charms, horoscopes, tarot cards and the like nothing more than entertainment. Occult practices are not a game, but a trap. And once a person is ensnared, it is very hard to escape. Don't listen to the devil, who is able to transform himself into an angel of light (2 Corinthians 11:14). Remember, he is a liar and the father of lies (John 8:44).

HE'S DEFEATED BUT HE WON'T GIVE UP

Satan has been a deceiver and a rebel from the moment he came into existence. The Bible tells us that he managed to persuade two-thirds of the angels to follow him into rebellion against God. The rebellion was easily crushed and Satan and his followers were kicked out of heaven. Today he continues his war against God, but he is capable of nothing more than a terrorist attack now and then. He was utterly defeated when Christ rose from the dead and you might think of God as conducting "mop-up" operations to round-up and eliminate Satan's last remaining troops.

But although his rebellion against God is all but over, we put ourselves in danger if we underestimate his brilliance. He has fooled many otherwise brilliant men and women during his long career, including Adam and Eve in the Garden of Eden (And I believe that as the crown of God's creation, Adam and Eve were created with extraordinary intelligence.). And if it was so easy for the devil to fool Adam and Eve, just think how easy is it for him to deceive modern man, particularly this new woke crowd.

My heart literally aches for those who have believed his lies concerning supernatural matters. Take tarot cards, for example. Divination, which is derived from Latin "meaning to foresee," is forbidden in the Bible. In ancient days it was referred to as soothsaying. Fortune telling has been around since ancient times and it has evolved to include reading palms, tarot cards, star charts, tea leaves and more.

First Samuel 15:23 compares rebellion to the sin of divination. Luke recorded the time in Philippi when a young slave girl who had a spirit of witchcraft followed after Paul and Silas crying out, "these men are slaves of the Most-High God who are proclaiming to you a way of salvation." After many days, Paul commanded the demon to come out of the girl in Jesus's name. The young woman's masters were not at all happy with what Paul had done, because she "was bringing great profit to her masters by fortune telling."

HOW DO SMART PEOPLE FALL FOR SUCH HOOEY?

How do normal, God-fearing individuals get caught up in false beliefs? One bizarre cult that comes to mind is the Heavens Gate group, whose members were coaxed into committing suicide. They believed that after their deaths they would be taken aboard a spaceship (in spirit form?) and then would fly to heaven in the wake of the Hale-Bopp comet. Does this sound like a reasonable idea to you? It certainly doesn't to me, but dozens of bright well-educated young men and women fell for it. This illustrates that human beings can be very gullible. Those who get involved in such bizarre schemes are absolutely convinced that these practices will work. They bet their lives on them and lose.

Some of these people are seeking power, others peace, while still others simply are inquisitive. Whatever the case may be, the individuals who are involved in these cults believe there are no absolutes.

CHAPTER EIGHT
WHO DO YOU TRUST?

Too many people put their trust in the political party they belong to.

They think they are fine because they are Republicans or Democrats or because they watch FOX News or CNN. The problem is that these things can't save you. Jesus Christ is not a Republican or a Democrat. He is far to high and powerful to be stuck with a political label.

Now, I certainly believe that there are some issues where Jesus' views would be more in line with one party than the other. Consider abortion, for example. The Republican Party is fighting to end abortion, while the Democratic Party is "pro-choice." In this extremely important matter, I believe our Lord would stand squarely with the Republican Party. But we do our Lord an injustice if we think of Him as the leader of the Republican Party. He is the Lord of all!

Our politicians may fail us, even those we have admired for so many years but He will never fail us.

On the other hand, there is a Republican Congressman who has been caught in many lies on his own resume but who when confronted about this says simply, "everybody lies." Leaders of his own party have asked him to step down but he refuses to do so. My point is that deciding who to vote for is not always a black and white issue. Remember that the Bible says all human beings have fallen short of the glory of God. We are all sinners for whom Christ died, which means that all political parties have unregenerate sinners within their ranks.

Because this is true, we must be extremely thorough in our vetting process and remember that people do not change unless the Lord changes them. In addition to a strong moral and spiritual character, look for a strong and clear communication skill. This skill must include the real ability to be a great listener. He or she must be able to "connect" with others. In other words you want to vote for someone who is empathetic, who wants to serve others rather than build up his own power.

You also want to vote for someone who will focus on his or her constituents' needs and not his party-line objectives. At the end of the day, you want to know that your family is protected that the person you elected has courage and will take a position that protects your interests. You also want someone who is passionate about life and encourages family values.

I also believe that it's important to vote for someone who is respectful and patient with regard to their opponents. You certainly want someone who is strong and forceful, but not a bully who is disrespectful and is constantly putting others down instead of focusing on the issues. You want someone who is humble in the sense that they are completely transparent, honest, open and understanding.

My opinion, built on decades of experience is that the single most important issue is trust!

One misstep can follow a politician forever and can ruin an otherwise outstanding career. For example, you may remember when presidential candidate George H.W. Bush said, "read my Lips. No new Taxes!" He defeated Michael Dukakis in 1988 but was not re-elected in 1992 because he did in fact raise taxes. Trust was gone.

THE ONLY ONE YOU CAN TRUST

The truth is that there is only one person you can always trust and that is God Himself. He will never lie to you or make you a promise that

He won't fulfill. If God says something, you can take it to the bank. Back in the day, I often saw a bumper sticker that said "God said it. I believe it. And that settles it." I liked that a lot. My only problem with it is that if God said something, it's true whether or not we believe it!

In fact, nothing happens in this universe unless God allows it to happen. Somebody may ask, "do I mean to say that God allowed Hitler to kill six million Jews?" Yes, He allowed it, but that doesn't mean He caused it or that He wanted it to happen. We just have to trust Him and know that He can and will bring good out of even the most tragic situations. Yes, God does allow earthquakes, fires and floods that destroy homes and people, diseases that kill innocent children and so forth.

So why does a loving God allow bad things to happen to people? Not a new question, and the answer is not so simple to comprehend, especially for someone who sees his or her loved ones suffering. But the answer can be found in the exquisite poetry of the Lord's Prayer:

> "Our Father who is in heaven,
> Hallowed be Your name.
> Your kingdom come.
> Your will be done,
> On earth as it is in heaven.
> Give us this day our daily bread.
> And forgive us our debts, as we also
> have forgiven our debtors.
> And do not lead us into temptation, but deliver
> us from evil. For Yours is the kingdom and the
> power and the glory forever. Amen." (Matthew
> 6:9-13, NASB)

In this discourse from His Sermon on the Mount, Jesus tells us how God's kingdom really works. He not only lets us know how to pray, but assures us that God is in Heaven and that He is our Father. To His listeners, this was a revolutionary statement. The Jews of the first century saw God as a distant being, too exalted and high to be thought of as a Father. But in this passage, Jesus is saying that this is exactly who God is. He cares about us as if we are His children, and we are.

Think about the fact that the Creator of the universe is our Father. "Hallowed be thy name." God is holy and therefore we must be holy. How can a sinful man approach a holy God? He can't? It is only when we have been sanctified through the blood of Jesus that we can come before God and speak to him as one friend to another or as child to daddy, (Jesus referred to God as Abba, which basically means "daddy.").

Once you have surrendered your life to Christ, God no longer sees your sin. Instead, when He looks at you, He sees the righteousness of His Son, who committed no sin and bore our sins on the cross.

In Jeremiah 27:34, God gave man a promise that was fulfilled in the sacrificial death of His Son, Jesus:

"For I will forgive their iniquity, <u>and their sin I will remember no more,</u>" (emphasis mine). God literally puts His memory into a "no-re-membrance compartment." Once you receive His gift of salvation by surrendering yourself to Christ, God welcomes you into His family. Your prayers are now heard and Heaven awaits you.

CHAPTER NINE
A BOOK TO GUIDE YOU

In the book *The Defender* which is co-authored by many men and women, the question is asked "have you ever wondered how Napoleon was able to win so many battles?" Of all the books written about him, only a handful mention that he was obsessed with a volume called *The Book of Fate*. This is an ancient Egyptian Oracle that Napoleon used for personal and military decisions.

Napoleon was not the only world leader who went to the dark side to find power to defeat his enemies. It is said that many of Hitler's top aides were deeply involved in the occult. This may explain some of their hatred for the Jewish people, since Satan clearly hates the Jews and has tried on several different occasions to destroy them.

Unfortunately, the dark side has even entered into the American White House invited in by a number of our First Ladies. You may remember the stir that was created when it was revealed that Nancy Reagan was involved in astrology, to the point that she had a personal astrologer who drew up charts for her.

Other notables who brought the dark side into the White House include Jane Pierce, Mary Todd Lincoln, Edith Wilson, Grace Coolidge, Lady Bird Johnson, Eleanor Roosevelt and Jackie Kennedy. These women had one issue in common. They were all desperate to find out why loved ones in their families had died at an early age and whether those individuals were happy and well in the after-life.

It's interesting that mediums and occultists of various kinds often claim they are doing God's work. And yet, God's Book the Bible, has extremely harsh words for them. In Deuteronomy 18:9-12, God tells the Israelites:

> "When you enter the land which the LORD your God gives you, you shall not learn to imitate the detestable things of those nations. There shall not be found among you anyone who makes his son or his daughter pass through the fire, one who uses divination, one who practices witchcraft, or one who interprets omens, or a sorcerer, or one who casts a spell, or a medium, or a spiritist, or one who calls up the dead. For whoever does these things is detestable to the LORD..."

And again, in Leviticus 20:6, we read:

> *"As for the person who turns to mediums and to spiritists, to play the harlot after them, I will also set My face against that person and will cut him off from among his people."*

Why is God so strong in his condemnation of those who are involved in the occult? I believe there are at least two reasons. The first is that God expects us to look to Him for guidance and direction in our lives and not to mediums, horoscopes or things like Ouija Boards. The dead are not gods, and they are not to be worshiped as gods. Have you ever known someone who couldn't make a decision without consulting his horoscope? I have. Plus, there are entire cultures on this planet who worship their dead ancestors instead of God.

Another reason why God is against communication with the dead is that this is an area where Satan and his demons are heavily involved. They are adept at impersonating our dead friends and relatives and in using this deceit to lead people away from God. I would go so far as to say that if you have ever contacted the dead through a medium, a séance or even a Ouija Board, it is not your dead loved ones that you have been communicating with but rather, Satan and his demons.

It is easy to be fooled especially if you are desperate to hear from your dearly departed mom or dad, spouse, son or daughter again. Over the last few months I have seen a number of news stories about grandparents and parents being scammed out of their life savings through the use of Artificial Intelligence. What happens is that they get a call from a grandson or granddaughter (or other loved one) saying, "I'm in trouble and I need you to send me X thousand dollars immediately." The person being scammed thinks they recognize that voice. "This really is my grandson," they think. And so they send their savings never to see their money again.

Artificial Intelligence does an amazing job of imitating people's voices and Satan can do the same thing. We must be careful and be aware.

I have had people say to me, "I know the Bible says not to get involved with the occult, but why should I trust the Bible?" After all, it's just another book. What makes it so special?

Let me give you a few answers to that question:

- **The Bible was written by approximately 40 men over 1,600 years.** And yet it is a unified whole, presenting a cohesive account of God's dealings with mankind over the centuries. Some of these authors were shepherds and fishermen. Others like the Apostle Paul, were highly educated scholars. The first five books were authored by Moses, a great prophet who grew up in Pharaoh's court. Luke (who also wrote the book of Acts) was a medical doctor and Matthew collected taxes for the Roman government before he was called by Jesus to be a disciple. Three kings also contributed to the Bible, David, Solomon and Lemuel. It is truly amazing that such a diverse group of writers were in complete agreement with each other on such subjects as the nature of God and the problem of sin. If these men weren't guided by the Holy Spirit, you could expect their book to be all over the place.

To put this into perspective, let's imagine that King David was in California when he wrote one of his Psalms and 800 years later a prophet in Israel wrote the exact same thing even though he had never seen what David wrote and there were no telephones, faxes or other modern means of communication. Impossible? Nothing is impossible with God. The writers of the Bible could not interact in any way, yet they wrote in absolute harmony. As Paul told his young protégé, Timothy, "All scripture is inspired by God and profitable for teaching, for reproof, for correction, for training in righteousness" (2 Timothy 3:16).

- **History supports the Bible.** Over 50 years ago, Josh McDowell wrote a terrific book called *Evidence that Demands a Verdict*. In his book, McDowell presented many examples where the Bible had been proven correct in areas where "scholars" had long considered it to be wrong. They said the Bible was wrong about certain dates. But archaeological discoveries proved that the Bible got it right. Other experts said that some of the characters mentioned in the Bible didn't really exist. Then legal documents were found in which these people were mentioned. There are many other similar examples in McDowell's book.

In 1999, McDowell came out with a follow-up book, *New Evidence that Demands a Verdict*, in which he talked about new discoveries that had further verified the Bible's accuracy in historical matters. In 2017, an expanded version of *Evidence that Demands a Verdict* was written by McDowell and his son Sean who is a PhD. I wholeheartedly recommend these books, which will give any reader a deeper understanding and appreciation of God's Word.

Keep in mind that history is the fulfillment of Bible prophecy. In the fourth chapter of the book of Daniel you can read about Nebuchadnezzar, the king of Babylon, who was so filled with pride that he thought he controlled the world. God dealt with his arrogance by causing him to lose his mind. For seven years, the once-proud king lived like an animal crawling on all fours and eating grass to survive. His attitude caused God to cut him down to size before he was eventually healed and restored to his throne. Check this out in your history books where the story of Nebuchadnezzar's illness is verified. God is always in control, not any man.

- **The Bible contains over seven thousand promises** and the apostle Paul says "they are all guaranteed." Because God is the giver of these promises, that statement is 100 percent correct. As 2 Peter 1:19 says, "So we have the prophetic word made more sure, to which you do well to pay attention as to a lamp shining in a dark place, until the day dawns and the morning star arises in your hearts."

Here are just a few of the thousands of promises of God that are found throughout the Bible.

God promises eternal life to you and everyone else who accepts Jesus Christ as Lord and Savior.

John 3:16 says, "For God so loved the world, that He gave His only begotten Son, that whoever believes in Him shall not perish, but have eternal life," (I think this is one of the verses that just about everybody knows and because of this, we may tend to take it for granted. We need to let this sink in and think about the amazing truth John is sharing here.).

He promises to restore your strength when you wait upon Him.

In Isaiah 40:31, we read,

"Yet those who wait for the LORD
Will gain new strength;
They will ⌈mount up with wings like eagles,

They will run and not get tired,
They will walk and not become weary."

He promises to give you rest when you're weary.

Matthew 11:28-30: "Come to Me all you who are weary and heavy-laden, and I will give you rest. Take My yoke upon you and learn from Me, for I am gentle and humble in heart, and you will find rest for your souls. For My yoke is easy and My burden is light."

He promises that when you resist the devil, he will flee from you.

James 4:7-8 says, "Submit therefore to God. Resist the devil and he will flee from you. Draw near to God and He will draw near to you."

He promises that He will never leave you nor forsake you.

Hebrews 13:5: "Make sure that your character is free from the love of money, being content with what you have; for He Himself has said, "I will never desert you, nor will I ever forsake you . . ."

He promises that He will always love you.

Isaiah 54:10: "For the mountains may be removed and the hills may shake, But My loving kindness will not be removed from you, and My covenant of peace will not be shaken, says the LORD who has compassion on you."

God has prepared a place in heaven for all who believe in His Son and that includes you.

John 14:1-3: "Do not let your heart be troubled; believe in God, believe also in Me. In My Father's house are many dwelling places; if it were not so, I would have told you; for I go to prepare a place for you. If I go and prepare a place for you, I will come again and receive you to Myself, that where I am, there you may be also."

As I said previously, these are only a fraction of the promises of God included in the Bible. Promises made to all those who have accepted Jesus Chris as Lord and Savior.

THE BIBLE IS FULL OF PROPHECIES, MANY OF WHICH HAVE ALREADY BEEN FULFILLED.

God gave man prophecy to prove that the Bible is true and written by the Holy Spirit. The Bible gives names of specific kings 175 years before they were born and mentions the battles they will fight. In fact, one-fifth of the Bible consists of prophecies like these:

Some 700 years before Christ was born, the prophet Micah wrote that he would be born in Bethlehem (**Micah 5:2**).

The prophet Zechariah, writing 800 years before the birth of Jesus, said that the Messiah would ride into Jerusalem on a colt (**Zechariah 9:9**). The fulfillment of this prophecy is recorded in all four of the Gospels: Matthew, Mark, Luke and John.

Zechariah also wrote that Christ would be betrayed by a friend (**Zechariah 11:12,13**). This prophecy was fulfilled when Judas Iscariot turned Jesus over to the Roman authorities for 30 pieces of silver.

It was prophesied that Jesus would be born of the seed of Abraham, that his mother would be a virgin and that He would one day would be scourged and put to death taking the penalty for our sins upon Himself (**Isaiah 53**).

Remember that only God can see the future. That's because He holds all of history in His hands. Put your faith in God, not in Nostradamus, Jeanne Dixon or whoever the latest celebrity fortune teller may be.

Throughout the Bible, there are many scriptures that support the authority and truth of the scriptures. Just look at what has taken place in the last century. We have seen the development of the atom bomb and other nuclear weapons that make it possible for the terrible destruction talked about in the book of Revelation to take place.

We have also seen the re-establishment of Israel after she was destroyed and the Jews were scattered over 2,000 years ago.

We have also witnessed the return of millions of Jews to the Promised Land, an event that is widely prophesied throughout the Old Testament (**See Ezekiel 37:21-22 for example.**).

On May 14, 1948, Israel was resurrected and soon after this it was filled with people who were speaking Hebrew, celebrating Jewish Feast Days and eating kosher foods. This is a miracle for sure. Normally, ten short years after a nation is overrun by an enemy the people no longer speak their own language or celebrate their culture. This makes the rebirth of Israel all the more amazing. Here are some of the other marvels we've seen within the last 100 years.

Supersonic rockets have allowed us to go to the moon and install satellites to further develop man's technology.

Computers have changed the landscape in all areas, especially in the fields of military and medicine.

Advancements in communication have made it possible for us to talk to people on the other side of the world instantaneously. Television brings war, natural disasters and other historical events right into our living rooms as they happen.

Breakthroughs in medicine have enabled us to defeat many diseases that were once deadly; however, it seems that almost every time one disease is defeated a brand-new one rears its ugly head. And, of course, some illnesses—like cancer and heart disease still kill thousands of people each day.

Unfortunately, despite the advances we have seen in medicine, technology and communications, the 21st century has also brought many negatives that are foretold in the Bible. For example, Jesus said that the last days would see an increase in wicked behavior. Anybody who doesn't believe this is happening all around us must have his or her eyes closed. Speaking from the Mount of Olives concerning the last days our Lord said, "because lawlessness is increased, most people's love will grow cold" (Matthew 24:12).

Jesus also talked about our overindulgence of food, drink and sex. "For as in those days before the flood they were eating and drinking, marrying and giving in marriage, until the day that Noah entered the ark, and they did not understand until the flood came and took them all away; so will the coming of the Son of Man be" (Matthew 23:38-39).

Sex today is glorified and marketed in films, on TV,

in pornographic magazines, in songs and in the promotion of the homosexual agenda extramarital affairs. All of this has helped drive the divorce rate up to the point where a staggering one out of two marriages fail. Many individuals who do not want the stigma of "divorce" have turned to "open marriages."

Read these words from the apostle Paul to his young friend, Timothy and see if they don't reflect the world we live in today:

> "But realize this, that in the last days difficult times will come. For men will be lovers of self, lovers of money, boastful, arrogant, revilers, disobedient to parents, ungrateful, unholy, unloving, irreconcilable, malicious gossips, without self-control, brutal, haters of good, treacherous, reckless, conceited, lovers of pleasure rather than lovers of God; holding to a form of Godliness, although they have denied its power; avoid such men as these" (2 Timothy 3:1-5).

If you still have any doubts as to whether the Bible is the Word of God; I urge you to look around and compare what you see to what was prophesied by the writers of the Bible. I'm pretty sure you'll decide the Bible was written by men who were inspired by God!

CHAPTER TEN

MORE ON THE DANGEROUS WORLD OF THE OCCULT

It's sad, but I am convinced that most people don't really care about their spiritual life. They are too busy seeking after the pleasures this life offers. God created us with sensors that tell us when we are hungry, when we are thirsty and when we need to some time for rest and sleep. Men are also hard-wired for reproduction. Women are also sex oriented, especially when they are interested in reproducing.

Animals on the other hand are driven by instinct. Woven into their DNA is the drive to eat and reproduce. Nimrod, his wife Semiramis and their son Tammuz where like animals in that they were driven by instinct rather than the Spirit of God. They were only interested in the things of this world. They always chose sin over righteousness.

God's desire was to change the natural man into a spiritual man. God exchanges the natural (Adam) for the spiritual (Christ). The Bible says, "As in Adam all die, so in Christ all will be made alive" (1 Corinthians 15:22).

Legend has it that Semiramis had a child through an adulterous affair while married to Nimrod. It is further understood that Nimrod died a violent death in an effort to retain power. In order for Semiramis to continue as a goddess she contrived a story that Nimrod had been resurrected. As a consequence, many false religions were birthed and all of these adopted different names for this mother-son duo. Paul describes this pagan worship of the creation in Romans 1:22-25.

According to 19th century theologian Alexander Hislop, writer of the book "The Two Babylons"[8] Semiramis invented polytheism to reinforce her pagan ideas. Her legacy for the modern world is lust! She did everything she possibly could to retain her position of power as well as keep her son on the throne.

In many ways, our world is following in the footsteps of this self-consumed woman.

TOLERANCE, THE NEW RELIGION

Our present society accepts no religion as right. In fact, the more tolerant your religion, the bigger the crowds you will draw. Cults hang on to their members by isolating them, showering them with love and keeping them immersed in cult philosophy. Often, they are able to keep a grip on their recruits by appealing to their interest in self-improvement.

Some people get trapped in cults simply because they are looking for structure or a sense of belonging. But as God says, speaking through the prophet Hosea "My people perish for lack of knowledge" (Hosea 4:6). No matter how it happens, you must understand God does not want His elect fooling around with teachings or things that come from demons. Satan's evil tricks and deceptions are designed for the purpose of getting you to take your eyes off of Jesus. Never forget, you are not wrestling with flesh and blood but "against principalities, against powers, against the rulers of the darkness of this world, against spiritual wickedness in high places" (Ephesians 6-11-12).

In their book, *Entertaining Spirits Unaware* David Benoit and Eric Barger write, "though the large percentage of those who operate in the occult kingdom have been cleverly brought to believe that there is no devil and what they practice is not satanic in nature, the fact remains that God, in His Word, clearly denounces each and every major New

---

[8] Hislop, Alexander, "The Two Babylons" (London:S.W. Partridge & Company) 1871

Age and occult practice in the world today. And if indeed the Bible is the truth, God verifies His warnings about the occult again and again through the words of His chosen servants. This culminates with Jesus Christ and the apostles identifying Satan as the enemy of our souls, the father of lies and as a creature resembling a savage lion seeking whom he may devour. So is astrology Satan worship? Not in the classic definition, but who gets the glory in the end? The devil himself. So is there any difference? No. The tragic end result is the same: "eternal judgement and separation from God." [9]

If you truly care about your eternity and take the time to read the Bible, you will see clearly that Christians should not take an interest in anything performed or spoken by soothsayers, witches or any occultist (Deuteronomy 18:10-12). History documents several world leaders who were reliant on words spoken by fortune tellers. Hitler definitely was one who relied upon the astrologers and there are many others.

Authors Benoit and Barger write that divination is not a gift. Despite what the psychic hotlines claim, there are no gifted psychics. There are however, demons that possess and consequently act like they are gifted people. The fate of all these is told in Revelation 21:7-8 and that is to suffer the pain of the fire that burns forever.

NO POWER IN THE STARS

Astrology is another forbidden practice. From the time of Nimrod, man has been obsessed with trying to find out what will take place in the future. In the modern world when science tells us what stars really are and we ought to know that there is nothing magical about them, astrology is still very big business. According to a recent poll, one of every four American adults say they trust in astrology. The number is even higher for adults under 30, with 37 percent saying they believe their lives are guided by the stars. The poll also found that

---

[9] Benoit, David and Barker, Eric, "Entertaining Spirits Unaware," (Oklahoma City:Hearthstone Publishers) 2001

only 51 percent of Americans say they don't believe in astrology with the remainder undecided.[10] No wonder every daily newspaper in the United States carries a horoscope (Incidentally, the same poll found that Republicans were less likely to vote for someone who believed in astrology.).

God minces no words. Speaking through the prophet Isaiah, he says, "you are wearied with your many counsels; Let now the astrologers, those who prophecy by the stars, those who predict by the new moons, Stand up and save you from what will come upon you; behold they have become like stubble, fire burns them; they cannot deliver themselves from the power of the flame. . ." (Isaiah 47:13-14).

As for the Bible, it flat-out condemns astrology.

NO "ENCHANTERS" IN GOD'S KINGDOM

Deuteronomy also has harsh words for people it calls "enchanters." This is a strange word, but essentially it refers to one who casts spells, a practice that is common in many countries today. Witches and enchanters are pretty much the same thing. Actually, witchcraft has been around for thousands of years. Helen Berger wrote the following in the September 2021 edition of *The Conversation*:

"Wicca and Witchcraft are part of the larger contemporary pagan movement, which includes druids and heathens among others."

All of these movements base their practices on pre-Christian religions and cultures. Witchcraft is rebellion plain and simple. It's man's desire to control the world in which he lives, instead of relinquishing control to God. This actually was man's sin in the garden of Eden. It was also Satan's motive for leading a revolt in heaven. And sad to say, it is the way of life for millions and millions of people who will face the

---

[10] YouGov.com/entertainment/articles/ "One in four Americans say they believe in astrology", accessed September 11, 2023

Great White Throne judgement which is discussed in the 21st chapter of Revelation. There, they will learn that they have been sentenced to pain and suffering for all eternity.

Wicca differs from mainstream Christianity in that it celebrates a goddess as well as a god. The emphasis is on direct spiritual experience and Wiccans are known as practitioners rather than believers. According to *Encyclopedia Britannica*, witchcraft is the practice of magic especially for evil purposes.

Is there a difference between New Agers and Wiccans? *Entertaining Spirits Unaware* says that the main difference is that "New Agers" practice their beliefs singularly and not in covens or groups. There are many similarities, such as communication with spirits for power and direction and using occult practices such as worshipping the earth. The book goes on to say, "perhaps the main difference is that witches and warlocks view their roots in Europe, New Agers on the other hand see their teaching from Eastern European Mystics."

Either way they are both dealing with demons. So you have a clear understanding of the Wicca religion, it is a pagan religion influenced by the ancient occult. It's also a new religious movement that draws on a secret society devoted to the study of "Occult Hermeticism." This Hermeticism is attributed to the teachings of Hermes in 300 BCE. Since Hermes was a mystical Greek god, all his writings were done by Thoth (scribe of the gods).

What do witches believe? Benoit and Barger write,

"Witches claim not to believe in the devil, because he is a biblical person. Instead, they communicate with and claim to manipulate spirits from another dimension."

Years ago, NBC's "Sunday Today" program featured a story about Laurie Cabot, who had been appointed by then Massachusetts' governor Michael Dukakis as official Witch of Salem. On that show she tried unsuccessfully to conjure spirits. In this ceremony, using a pentacle as an amulet (a conduit for power) Cabot chanted, "Earth. . .Air. . .Fire. . .Water. . . Great Spirit, I invoke the god and goddess within my body."

I don't really know what Ms. Cabot expected to happen, but as far as the cameras could tell nothing did. The lights didn't even flicker.

New Agers have been telling us for years to look inside ourselves for enlightenment, wisdom, or power. The same could be said of Witchcraft. Cabot prayed to five spirits, the spirits of Earth, Wind, Fire, Water and the Great Spirit. This is a perfect example of paganism through the ages.

The NBC show seemed to approach the whole idea of witchcraft as it if it were fun and games, something cute. But getting involved with demons is not a game. It is a deadly serious business. It is fighting against God and nothing good can ever come from that.

Before we move on from the subject of Wicca and Witchcraft, there are two more points I'd like to mention:

1. According to Benoit and Barger, Witchcraft is a religion. The U.S. Chaplain's manual states that it is a religion and identifies Wiccan holidays: spring equinox, summer solstice, autumn equinox, winter solstice, candlemas, May eve, lamas, and Halloween.

2. I'd like to talk about the nature of Feminism, which is often an important component of Witchcraft. The *Encyclopedia Britannica* defines it as "the advocacy of women's rights on the basis of equality of the sexes." Simply stated, it is about both genders having equal rights and opportunities. In other words, no gender is valued less than the other. The truth is that it is impossible for men and women to be equal in every respect. Humans are not machines. You cannot expect a five-foot-one-inch female to compete against NBA legend Lebron James for the center position. God created Adam, and He created Eve and He created them in His image and likeness. In other words in God's eyes,

men and women are equal. The Bible says, "There is neither Jew nor Greek, there is neither slave nor free, there is neither male nor female; for you are all one in Jesus Christ" (Galatians 3:28). The laws in the Old Testament, that were written to protect women were based on a society that did not recognize women as equals. Yes, men and women are equals. But that does not mean that we are the same. We have different strengths that complement each other, and this is a display of God's wisdom.

YESTERDAY AND TODAY

I believe that pagan practices and beliefs are strangling our young people. And yet, God forbid that "Big Brother" should hear of any public school teacher who talks about Christmas. Any remarks concerning Christ are off limits, yet everyone can tolerate and embrace Islam, Astrology, Wicca, witchcraft, etc.

Far too many of today's parents don't make time for explaining truths to their children. Money is their god! Therefore, witchcraft and other pagan beliefs are defying Christianity. And even as this happens, practitioners of these new-age religions say that we Christians are "intolerant" because we won't turn our backs on what the Bible says, join hands with them and dance together in the light of the moon. Unfortunately, those who try to be "tolerant" are watering down the truth and this is the first step on the way to losing your bearings spiritually.

What does the Lord think about all this? Read 1 Samuel 15:23 in the New Living Testament: "Rebellion is as sinful as witchcraft, and stubbornness as bad as worshiping idols. . . ." And the NIV reads, "For rebellion is like the sin of divination, and arrogance like the evil of idolatry . . . ."

So you understand exactly what is meant, rebellion is an attitude that contradicts authority. Adam and Eve were rebellious. In this state they could not receive the gifts God gives to those who are obedient.

Those who live in rebellion should expect to be delivered into the hands of their enemies (Nehemiah 9:26). A rebel will live out his or her days in a dry land (Psalm 68:6). Rebellion can shorten your life and leave you literally fighting against God (Isaiah 63:10). And that's one fight nobody can win!

WHAT ABOUT YOUR LUCKY RABBIT'S FOOT?

As you were reading the above material, you may have been thinking, "This has nothing to do with me. I don't cast spells, believe in amulets or practice new-age religion in any way."

But what about charms like a lucky rabbit's foot, a four-

leaf clover or a horseshoe posted over a door so it can pour

out blessings onto your home. Do you carry a Saint Christopher medal to keep you safe when you travel or have you ever buried a statue of St. Joseph in your yard to help you sell your home? All of these practices are based on superstition and magic and they are not compatible with the Word of God.

This is true of anything that is worn by people to ward off evil or simply to guarantee good luck. I think of the Scapular. According to the book "Roman Catholicism" by Boettner, the scapular was invented in 1287 by an English monk named Simon Stock. Catholic tradition says that Mary, the mother of Jesus, appeared to him in celestial splendor. She was carrying a scapular and commissioned him to take it as a sign of the Carmelite Order to which he belonged. It was to be worn at all times and never taken off. If worn at time of death, it was a direct pass to heaven. Reading the scapular that was issued to our armed forces in World War Two we find, "Whosoever Dies Clothed In This Scapular Shall Not Suffer Eternal Fire." Think about this, when you die wearing this pagan amulet you go directly to heaven.

RUBBISH!!

If this were true, than why did Christ have to die on the cross? This teaching about the scapular belittles the sacrifice that Christ made on our behalf. Other such amulets would include so-called pieces of wood from the cross on which Christ died, bones from saints (most of these bones are from animals) and various types of medals.

You would be amazed to see how many "so called" Christian amulets are to be found in Christian book stores. Good luck statues, protective angel charms, etc. But your life has nothing to do with luck! God is in control, not some man-made trinket. God has a different idea.

> Daniel 5:23 says, "But you have exalted yourself against the Lord of heaven; and they have brought the vessels of His house before you; and you and your nobles, your wives and your concubines have been drinking wine from them; *and you have praised the gods of silver and gold, of bronze, iron, wood and stone, which do not see, hear or understand. But the God and all your ways, you have not* glorified" (Emphasis mine).

It's critical for you to understand that every breath you take has been ordained by God. In the scripture quoted above, we see Belshazzar (king of Babylon, grandson of Nebuchadnezzar and son of Nitocris) drinking from gold goblets held sacred by the Jews. It was like a slap directly in in the face of the Creator of the universe. It was at this moment that a disembodied hand appeared and began to write on the wall: **MENE, MENE, TEKEL, UPHARSIN.**

When no one in the king's service could translate the message written on the wall, Daniel was brought in to interpret:

"This is the interpretation of the message: 'MENĒ'—God has numbered your kingdom and put an end to it. 'TEKĒL'—you have been weighed on the scales and found deficient. 'PERĒS'—your kingdom has been divided and given to the Medes and Persians."

Belshazzar's last breath came that evening.

As the Apostle Paul wrote: "Do not be deceived, God is not mocked; for whatever a person sows, this he will also reap" (Galatians 6:7).

CHAPTER ELEVEN

WHICH WAY WILL AMERICA GO?

"The more sinful a generation becomes, the less truth the people will tolerate!"

If you are still on the fence about the Bible and whether it is the inspired Word of God, I urge you to make a leap of faith and choose belief in the Bible. I believe there is more than enough evidence to support the Bible's claim to be God's Holy Book. But I also believe it comes down to a decision everyone has to make. Will you believe? Or will you refuse to believe?

Based on the fact that our world and more specifically our country have moved to extreme levels of materialism and sexual perversion, I believe it's safe to say we are living in times that are very similar to those that took place prior to the Great Flood.

As a younger man, I knew there were two highways through life: the narrow road and the wide road. In those days, I wasn't really sure how important my choice was until I read and re-read the following scriptures:

> "Enter by the narrow gate; for the gate is wide, and the way is broad that leads to destruction, and many are those who enter by it. For the gate is small, and the way is narrow that leads to life, and few are those who find it" (Matthew 7:13-14).

And again:

> "Not everyone who says Lord, Lord, will enter the kingdom of heaven, but the one who does the will of My Father who is in heaven._On that day many will say to Me, 'Lord, Lord did we not prophecy in your name, and cast out demons in your name, and do many mighty works in your name?' And then will I declare to them, I never knew you; depart from Me, you workers of lawlessness" (Matthew 7:21-23).

Does God want us to vote for a Democrat or a Republican? Neither. He is looking for a Theocrat. In other words, someone who desires to follow His will and who is walking on the narrow way that leads to life. Too many among us today have rejected God or remade Him into our own image.

Frank Sinatra was one of the most popular entertainers of the last century. He sold millions of records, appeared in movies and performed in front of sold-out audiences around the world.

In an interview with Playboy Magazine, Sinatra was asked if he believed in God. His answer could have been directly from a pantheistic handbook. His thoughts were, "I think I can sum up my religious feelings in a couple of paragraphs. First I believe in you and me, I believe in nature, in the birds, the sea, the sky, in everything I can see or there is evidence for, but I don't believe in a personal God to whom I look for comfort... I'm not unmindful of faith, I'm for anything that gets you through the night, be it prayer, tranquilizers or a bottle of Jack Daniel's. . .." At the end of his life, Sinatra was reacquainted with the religion of his youth. He was a practicing Roman Catholic and was buried in that faith.

As for Oprah, she created her own "form" of Christianity. She grew up Baptist, but on her show often criticized orthodox Christianity. On April 24, 2008, Oprah said, "I am my own salvation. Let me remember there is no sin, heaven is not a location, but refers to the inner realm of consciousness."

Before you vote for somebody, ask where he or she stands on matters of faith. You must be truthful to God so do not deceive yourself. Make sure you are aware of the platform your candidate stands upon. Is he or she in favor of abortion? Homosexuality? Transgenderism?

The point is that if your candidate is in the Democratic Party, you can be sure that they support all of these things because they are in the Democratic platform. You can trick yourself by saying, "But my candidate is a Christian and would never side with issues God is against, plus he or she has a great family and they go to church," but you would be wrong.

The book of James says, "So for one who knows the right thing to do and does not do it, for him it is sin" (James 4:17). If you are a Christian, you must be prepared to respond to evil i.e., *fight the good fight*. Like Jesus, James' intention is to make obedience to God our highest priority. In other words, be a "do-er" of the Word and not just a reader of the Word. Be cognizant of who you must answer to in the end and be aware that the end (death) gets to you a lot quicker than you think it will.

THE EMPTINESS OF LIFE WITHOUT BELIEF

In the Bible book of Ecclesiastes, "the preacher," whose real name was Solomon, demonstrates the futility of a life lived without an eternal perspective. He writes that a life dedicated to the pursuit of earthly goals brings major disappointment and a feeling of emptiness.

"I became great and increased more than all who preceded me in Jerusalem. My wisdom also stood by me. All that my eyes desired I did not refuse them. I did not withhold my heart from any pleasure, for my heart was pleased because of all my labor and this was my reward for all my labor. Thus, I considered all my activities which my hands had done and the labor which I had exerted, and behold all was vanity and striving after wind and there was no profit under the sun" (Ecclesiastes 2:9-11).

In the book of Ecclesiastes, the idiom "under the sun" means "God is left out." Today we call it self-centeredness. After all of his searching and striving, what did "the preacher" decide?

> "The conclusion, when all has been heard, is: fear God and keep His commandments, because this applies to every person. For God will bring every act to judgment, everything which is hidden, whether it is good or evil" (Ecclesiastes 12:13-14).

You see, as humans, we all want to be happy. The problem is that unless we understand that God can make us happy, we look in all the wrong places for it: sexual gratification, wealth, power. Now, there is nothing wrong with any of these things. God created them all. But he intends sexual gratification to be the result of love and devotion between one man and one woman. He gives us wealth in order that we can be a force for good in the world, not so that we can buy the things we need to satisfy our own selfish desires. And power can be a wonderful thing when it is desired for the right reason and that is to make the world a better place.

Those who are successful in politics obtain great power. In fact, there is no more powerful person on the earth than the President of the United States. But the question is, why does somebody who has decided to go into politics want power? Did he choose a political career because he has a desire to make the world a better place? Or does he want power because it will give him prestige, name recognition and enable him to throw his weight around.

How can you know if someone is motivated by the wrong reasons? You can watch them. Listen to what they say. Do their words and actions line up? You can also pray that God will reveal the truth to you. If you ask with a sincere heart, He will respond.

CHAPTER TWELVE

WHOSE KINGDOM ARE YOU BUILDING?

When He gave His Sermon on the Mount, Jesus issued this challenge to His listeners:

"Seek first His kingdom and His righteousness and all these [good] things will be added unto you" (Matthew 6:33).

I admit that it is not always easy to put God's kingdom first. In fact, we can only do it with His help. Human beings are naturally selfish creatures and so until we surrender our lives to Christ, most of us are working on our own kingdoms. It's only when we are born-again and surrender our will to His that we get our priorities straight and begin putting God's kingdom first.

Jesus told us on many occasions that we are to die to our own desires and submit to God. The purpose of your life is not to fulfill your will but God's will. Fortunately, we can trust Him and know that the life He wants for us is better than anything we could build for ourselves.

Abraham Lincoln once said that he would never pray for God to bless His side in an issue. Instead, he would seek God's will and strive to be on God's side. I like that. We should always seek to build God's kingdom by being on His side in everything we do and that includes the votes we cast for various candidates, propositions and other issues.

We should always ask ourselves, "How does God feel about this issue? How would Jesus vote?"

Keep in mind that Christians are to have an eternal perspective. As Paul writes, "For momentary, light affliction is producing for us an eternal weight of glory far beyond all comparison, while we look not at the things which are seen, but at the things that are not seen; for the things which are seen are temporal, but the things which are not seen are eternal" (2 Corinthians 4:18).

WILL YOU BE A DISCIPLE?

I said earlier that if you continue in the Lord's Word and obey, you will be a disciple of God. Jesus tells us, "If you abide in My word then you are truly disciples of Mine; and you shall know the truth, and the truth shall make you free" (I John 8:31-32).

Please don't tell yourself you can't surrender your life to Christ right now because you're having too much fun experiencing all the pleasure that sin has to offer. There is nothing as joyous as a life that has been surrendered to Christ and the more time you spend in sin, the harder it will be for you to get free. You see, there is no such thing as a "little sin" and if you think that's the case, you are fooling yourself. The man who sins does not do what he likes, but what sin likes. He is a captive to his sin. Sin becomes an unbreakable habit and thus, no man who sins can be free! Yet Jesus says that knowing the truth will set you free, and goes on to explain, "I am the way, the truth and the life" (John 14:6).

If you are a Roman Catholic, you may believe in "venial sins" or as Catholicism teaches, "lesser sins," which do not result in complete separation from God. According to Catholic teaching, venial sins do not break your friendship with God, only slightly injuring your relationship with Him. The word venial means "forgivable."

All of this is untrue. I know that for a fact because if it were true Jesus would have told us! Our sins put Jesus on the cross and they are forgivable only through his shed blood.

The Catholic Church also teaches about a place called Purgatory, where those who aren't quite good enough to make it into heaven will go when they die. Here they say, souls will suffer through long years of torment until their sins are purged and they are fit for heaven.

But where is this in the Bible? Where is there even a hint of such a place. There isn't one. If Purgatory existed, surely the prophets or apostles would have mentioned it. Purgatory, according to *Encyclopedia Britannica*, comes from a Latin verb meaning "to cleanse." According to Catholicism it's an actual place and until 1563, buying indulgences to commute the pain for one's loved ones in purgatory was outlawed.

The plain truth is that there are no second chances. God the Father gave us His only begotten Son and told us to believe in Him not to trust in our own efforts or believe the lies of Satan, such as that we will be given a second chance after we die. So do it right the first time, with Jesus as your Lord and Savior. And be darn sure you check whom you vote for.

Jesus says in Matthew 23:27, "Woe to you, teachers of the law and Pharisees, you hypocrites! You are like whitewashed tombs, which look beautiful on the outside but on the inside are full of dead men's bones and everything unclean." This is one of the seven woes Jesus pronounced on the religious leaders of His day as He confronted them on their hypocrisy. Basically, this speaks to a widespread spiritual condition of man: "You look good on the outside, but on the inside you are dead."

Your understanding will blossom once you are born again. Unfortunately, natural man cannot understand spiritual truths. We are in need of spiritual help and that help can only come when we surrender to Jesus Christ and are born again. I understand how difficult it may be for some people to make the decision to become a Christian.

I was raised and educated in Catholicism, so it was very difficult for me to understand that Christ is the focal point in Christianity. I prayed to Mary every day, but thought Jesus was beyond my pay grade. Don't get me wrong. I loved Jesus, but all through my early years the nuns and priests seemed to acknowledge Mary more and saying the rosary was a must before each football game. At the age of 25, I married a born-again believer named Mary who prayed for me incessantly and never gave up on me. I would say, "No need to pray. I know the Lord." But I didn't really know Him. Mary would put a book about new birth on my night table, hoping I would read it. Each evening I would take the book, open it to see if there was an imprimatur (official license by the Catholic Church allowing Catholics to read). When there wasn't, I refused to read. Many months passed and no imprimaturs were to be found. Then one evening Mary put, *The Born-Again Catholic* by Albert H. Boudreau on my nightstand. It had an imprimatur: Rev. James D. Niedergeses, Bishop of Nashville. I read or more accurately, devoured the book culminating with a prayer on page 153. The Lord knew the right person to get to me, my wife Mary who is a true saint and loves Jesus.

From the very first time we meet Satan in the Bible, he is always trying to twist the truth. He tells Adam and Eve that they won't die when they eat the forbidden fruit but rather become like God, knowing the difference between right and wrong, good and evil. He is right that they will not die immediately. And they do suddenly have an enhanced understanding of good and evil. But their sin opened the door and let death in, not just for the first couple but for every other human being who has ever existed and all the animals as well.

The Bible also tells us that after Jesus was baptized by His cousin John the Baptist, He went into the wilderness where He was tempted by Satan. Satan even used scripture in an attempt to get our Lord to turn His back on His calling. But he also twisted that scripture so that the real meaning was obscured (see Matthew 4:1-11).

Today, Satan is still in the practice of twisting and distorting the Word of God and he has taught his minions how to do the very same thing. Make no mistake, Satan knows the Bible. One of the very best ways to defeat him is to know it better than he does. That way, we will not fall for his distortions.

The person who wants to be close to God must spend time in His holy word, not only reading it, but meditating on it and letting its truths sink deep into the soul. And then living out its truths in his or her daily life.

WHAT DOES ALL OF THIS HAVE TO DO WITH YOUR VOTE?

We have explored some very important issues in our time together, including how Satan and his forces wage a war of deception that allows them to get a foothold in someone's life. If you are reading this and become very agitated or feel that you are in need of doing something every minute, then you owe it to yourself to learn how to accept and enjoy the peace the Lord wants for you: first, understand that the demonic world around us definitely exists and certainly hinders Christian growth and freedom, which undermines any peace one may have.

Keep in mind two important points:

1. God is in control.

2. Your struggle is against powers and principalities of darkness.

I urge you to keep the following Bible verses in mind at all times:

"Now the lord is the spirit, and where the Spirit of the Lord is, there is liberty" (2 Corinthians 3:17).

"And you will know the truth and the truth will make you free" (John 8:32).

Therefore, the first step toward freedom is "peace with God." Getting right with God is simply accepting His plan of salvation and not your own. Most of us have trouble accepting the fact that we are really sinners. We think, "How can God reject me? I go to church, I tithe, I give to the poor, I volunteer for helping in church, I am good to my neighbors, love my children and don't cheat on my wife."

But if we look closer, we can see the many ways we fall short of God's glory every day. We may exaggerate the truth or have selfish or lustful thoughts. We may tell "little white lies" when we think they will help us get out of trouble.

You see, we are all in need of a Savior! Only the love of Jesus and the sacrifice He paid for us, can save us from what we deserve which is eternity in hell.

Once you have accepted God's plan of salvation, then you are free to live in obedience to His will. In other words, when what we want is in alignment to God's will then we are truly free.

Here are some ways you can follow God's plan as you step into the voting booth.

SELECTION OF A CANDIDATE:

1. Ask yourself if the candidate you are going to vote for has an understanding of truth that syncs up with the Bible. Does he or she have good leadership abilities and are they taking a proper stance on present-day issues. If you have surrendered your life to Jesus, it's very important to ask the Holy Spirit for guidance.

2. Does your candidate possess and exercise Christian morals and Christian principles?

If you are a normal God-fearing person, you are more than likely fed up with the politics of today. Can your voice be heard? Can you explain how an individual like George Santos could lie his way into the

United States Congress? Explain to me why there is no consequences to his deception?

Godly wisdom is the application of truth! Scripturally, wisdom is a capacity of the mind that allows us to understand life from God's perspective. Solomon, in the book of Proverbs (chapter 4, verse 5) tells his readers to "get wisdom." In Ecclesiastes 7:23-24) he says, "I tested all this with wisdom, and I said "I will be wise," but it was far from me. What has been is remote and exceedingly mysterious. Who can discover it?

HERE'S HOW YOU CAN "GET WISDOM"

1. ***FEAR GOD:*** *"The fear of the Lord is the beginning of wisdom" (Proverbs 9:10)* This fear is Filial not Servile. Filial is respect and love, the type of "fear" you have for parents. Servile is they type of fear you might have for your jailer.

2. **Desire Wisdom: (Proverbs 2:4)** You must desire it with all your heart, per Solomon (Proverbs 2:4).

3. **Pray for Wisdom.** "But if any of you lacks wisdom, let him ask of God, who gives to all generously and without reproach, and it will be given to him" (James 1:5).

4. **Study God's Word:** "The Law. . .the testimony of the Lord is sure, making wise the simple" (Psalm 19:7).

TIME IS NOT ON MAN'S SIDE: ETERNITY COULD BE YOUR NEXT BREATH, SO WAKE UP!

I realize that some of you who are reading this think it is nonsense. But please answer this question as seriously and honestly as you can: what do you really think about heaven and hell?

Some will say there is no such place, in other words you live your life and then it's over. If that were true, why did you cry when your mom or dad or one of your siblings passed away. You cried because down deep in the reservoir of your being, you know they went somewhere. Their body was just a container for their soul, which has flown away.

Seriously, one certainty in life is death. Sooner or later it knocks on your door. Are you basing your eternity on what came out of a mind of man? And are you ready for that knock? Solomon wanted to know all about living and dying, he was wiser than all other men. When God asked him "ask what I shall give you" Solomon replied, "give your servant therefore an understanding mind to govern your people, that I may discern between good and evil, for who is able to govern this Your great people? (I Kings 3:9)" (Think about this, Solomon could have asked for anything, anything at all. What would you have chosen?). In the book of Ecclesiastes, we see Solomon searching for the meaning of life. He is not looking for help from the law or the Prophets, meaning he does not look to traditional religion. He searches the depths of human experiences and concludes the necessity for eternity. What he did was examine the emptiness and futility of life (This is something you do not have to explain to a retired person; they realize that they have been replaced by a newer 2.0 model and their name will not be remembered in ten years, let alone what they have accomplished.).

The bottom line is that the world teaches that nothing has meaning. Nothing matters! Since God will bring everything into the light and He will judge, Solomon concludes that "truth is everything." Ecclesiastes defends the life of faith from a loving God, yet points to a life of futility and foolishness without eternal perspective. Can anyone cope with living and not knowing where you are going? Solomon concluded that ALL earthly goods and blessings, when pursued as ends in themselves lead to emptiness and pain.

Whether you are a Democrat, Republican or Independent, pray that the Lord will give you wisdom regarding which lever to pull. Be sure you understand the platform on which you stand. God will never wink at sin. If He says a sin is an abomination, then believe it. You cannot take the path that says, "God knows I do not like this or that but He will understand why I voted the way I did." No, he will not and cannot understand because he is a holy God.

CHAPTER THIRTEEN
THE MOST IMPORTANT QUESTION EVER

Now that we have come to the end of our time together, I need to take care of some unfinished business.

I want you to ask yourself one very important question:

if you should die suddenly, what would become of you?

Ask yourself what your legacy would be for your family. Did anything you accomplished in your life really matter?

If you have accepted Jesus Christ as your Lord and Savior, then these words from the apostle Paul are for you:

"For we know that if the earthly tent (body) which is our home is torn down, we have a building from God, a house not made with hands, eternal in the heavens" (2 Corinthians 5:1).

Paul also writes that for the person who belongs to Christ,

"to be away from the body is to be at home with the Lord" (2 Corinthians 5:8).

In John 14:2-3, Jesus Himself says, "in my Father's house are many dwelling places; if it were not so, I would have told you; for <u>I go to prepare a place for you.</u>"

Think of it like this: your soul is your body, your tent. This tent is a fragile structure. Your death pulls it down but as a Christian you move immediately to your eternal home, heaven. Death is the tearing apart of what God joined together. Death is your enemy, it literally is the undoing of our nature.

Now, imagine you realize that each of your functions are ceasing to work as designed. You can no longer speak or see, walk nor eat, not even move the slightest muscle and eventually you will be unconscious. No human being in their right mind would want their soul to be separated from their body. Death basically tears the soul from the body, which is not a pleasant thought. As a matter of fact, it's a terrifying thought.

If you are one of those people who believe there is nothing after death, consider what I said previously. You are lost, destined for an eternity of hell. No resting place ever! Let that sink in.

As for Christians and believing Jews, there is an exchange and it happens instantaneously. You exchange the earthly tent for a heavenly building. The temporary for the eternal.

God didn't have to tell us anything about heaven. He could have simply said "trust Me and wait until you die." Instead, He gave humankind a hope that will be fulfilled in Christ.

WHAT ABOUT NON-BELIEVERS?

Most pagans believe in reincarnation. Ancient pagan men would support the dying individual by caressing them and encouraging them to discuss their fears and feelings about dying. Pagans see life and death as two sides of the same coin. Death is viewed as a form of shedding their skin, similar to a snake. In this way death becomes a symbol of life, a rebirth if you will.

Consider Wiccan traditions. They believe that the souls of the dead rest for a period of time in another world they call "Summerland," where the traumas of the past life are healed and the dead person is comforted in the arms of the goddess. Pagans worship people, animals and plants. Many believe that trees, forests, rivers, etc. have a life force, and need to be conserved.

Why am I saying all this if the subject of this book is Democracy? Simply stated, my hope is that you truly vet those you plan on voting for.

I also want to make sure that you have followed God's will, not only insofar as your votes are concerned but in a way that will benefit you in this life and in the life to come. 1 Timothy 2:4 says that God "desires all men to be saved and to come to the knowledge of the truth." The bottom line is that God wants you to spend eternity in heaven and whether you know it or not, you want to be there too. Please don't miss out. Death is inevitable, but annihilation is not. Surrender yourself to Him through faith in Jesus Christ and have the peace and pleasure of knowing that your future will be absolutely glorious!